MW01392631

WOOD'S WHISPERS
Echo through Time

Wood's Whispers
Echo Through Time
Copyright © 2024 by Glenn P. Wood. All rights reserved.

No part of this publication may be reproduced, stored in a retrieval system, or transmitted in any way by any means, electronic, mechanical, photocopy, recording, or otherwise without the prior permission of the author except as provided by USA copyright law.

The opinions expressed by the author are not necessarily those of Veritas Ink and Press

Veritas Ink and Press is committed to excellence in the publishing Industry.

Book Design copyright 2024 by Veritas Ink and Press & Glenn P Wood. All Rights Reserved.

Illustrated By: Glenn P. Wood

Published in the United States of America

Hardback ISBN : 979-8-3305-5904-6

DEDICATION

This book is dedicated to the trees that refresh our air, offer us shade, and—most importantly—provide the fine material used to expand our cultures, building our homes, ships, and mighty cathedrals.

To those remarkable trees that have served as milestones throughout my life, I owe my deep admiration for the natural world and the wisdom they inspire in me. Their silent presence reminds me of the urgent need to protect the environment for future generations.

I also dedicate this work to the memory of my father, William Henry Wood, whose legacy fostered my lifelong interest in wood and endowed me with the ability to commune with it.

FORWARD

The first volume of the Wood Whisperer's trilogy, titled *Messengers in Time*, contained eight short stories recounting events in the lives of historical boxes that traveled through time and space to arrive safely in the USA. They came from many distant lands, with some having lived for almost 400 years.

Whatever their age or origin, these boxes shared two things in common: they were made of different types of exotic woods, and they all eventually found sanctuary in my private collection of antique wooden boxes. Like me, these boxes have come to rest in their adopted home of America. The international success of these short stories inspired me to publish a follow-up account featuring ten additional boxes.

In *Echoes from the Past*, I gave equal importance to both antique and modern boxes, expanding the definition of what may be considered a 'box.' One such tale tells the story of little Carol Catley, a child prodigy violinist from Manchester, England, who became an international performer but ultimately died in obscurity in America. Her violin case narrates this story—a nod to my earlier work, *The Art & History of Violin Cases,* an eclectic piece of non-fiction that continues to spark interest and curiosity.

In *Wood's Whispers - Echo Through Time*, I have used antiques as conduits to explore profound themes such as immigration, luxury, revolution, sustainability, faith, and civil war. These deeper ideas subtly underpin the narrative, while the true protagonists are the ligneous treasures themselves. This collection culminates in the critically acclaimed story of the Sedan Box, where a 400-year-old survivor from the Chinese Ming dynasty warns of the perils of civil war.

While countless books have been written about trees and wood, rarely have they been given the chance to narrate their own stories through their interactions with humanity. In this collection, their tales reveal their rich encounters with people over the centuries, perhaps offering insights into our own nature in the process.

'The Wood Whisperer'
Aka Dr. Glenn P. Wood
York, PA, USA — September 2024

CONTENTS

THE TORTOISESHELL BOX (c. 1696)
Ink That Echoes Through Time 1
THE SANDALWOOD BOX (c. 1849)
Fragrance of Forgotten Sorrows 7
THE SAMURAI BOX (c. 1830)
Borders Crossed, Lives Changed 14
THE BIBLICAL BOX (c. 1990)
Cleopatra's Secret Treasure 19
THE MAHARAJA'S BOX (c. 1849)
The Raj's Untold Whispers 24
THE TSAR'S BOX (c. 1890)
Griffins and Lost Empires 29
THE NOMAD'S BOX (c. 1970)
Out of Africa, Into History 34
THE VIETNAM BOX (c. 1820)
Identity Lost, Truth Revealed 39
THE PALMWOOD BOX (c. 1920)
From Riches to Ruin 45
A PAGAN BOX (c. 1970)
A Prayer for Every Soul 54
THE SEDAN BOX (c. 1620)
Divided by Tyranny 62
THE TWO LOCK BOX (c. 1650)
Family Secrets, Locked Away 71

NB
The stories are presented in black text. Additional historical or technical information is provided in blue for those interested in further details. Readers may skip the blue sections if they wish to focus solely on the narrative.

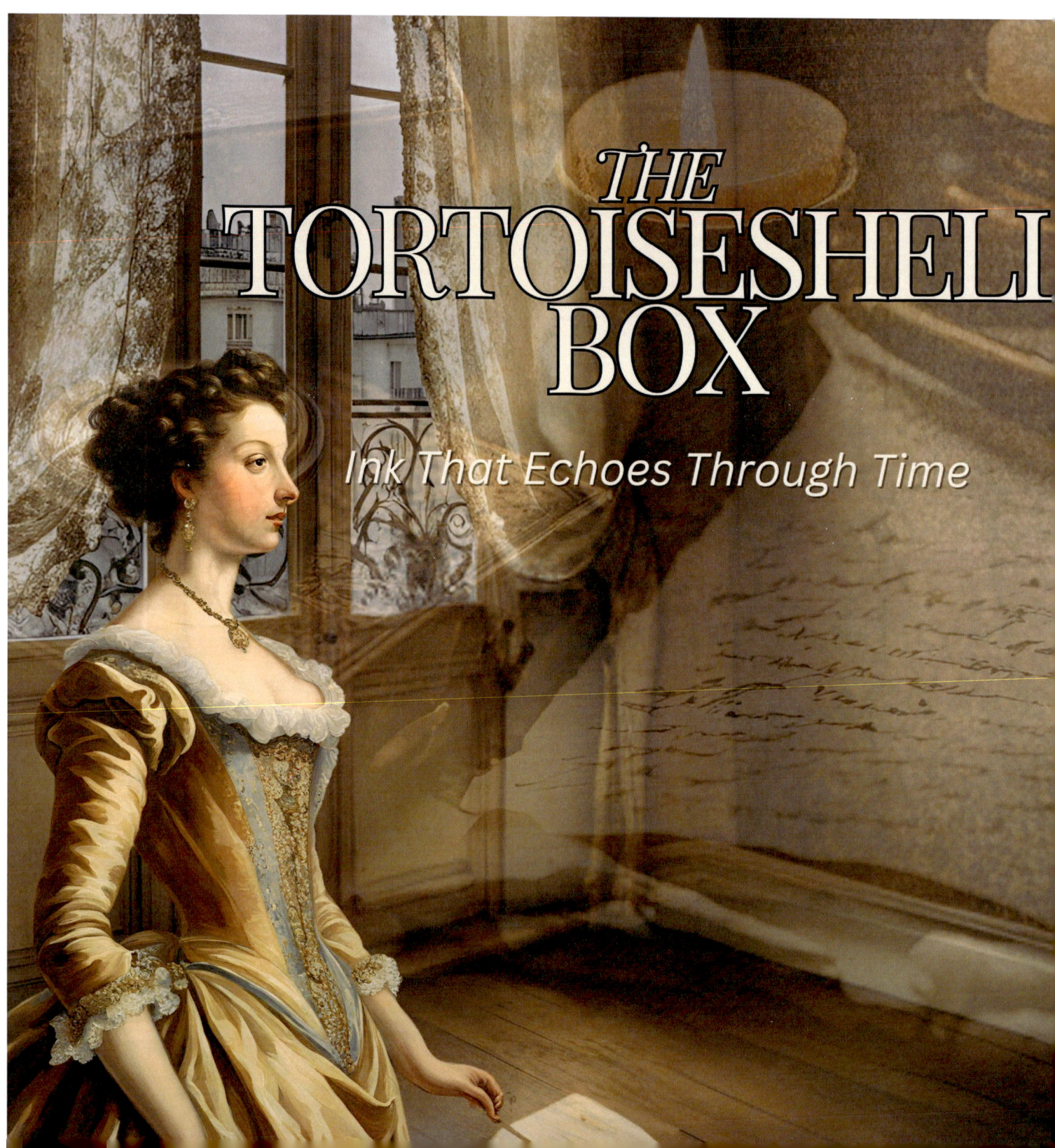

THE TORTOISESHELL BOX

Ink That Echoes Through Time

THE TORTOISESHELL BOX (c. 1696)
Ink That Echoes Through Time

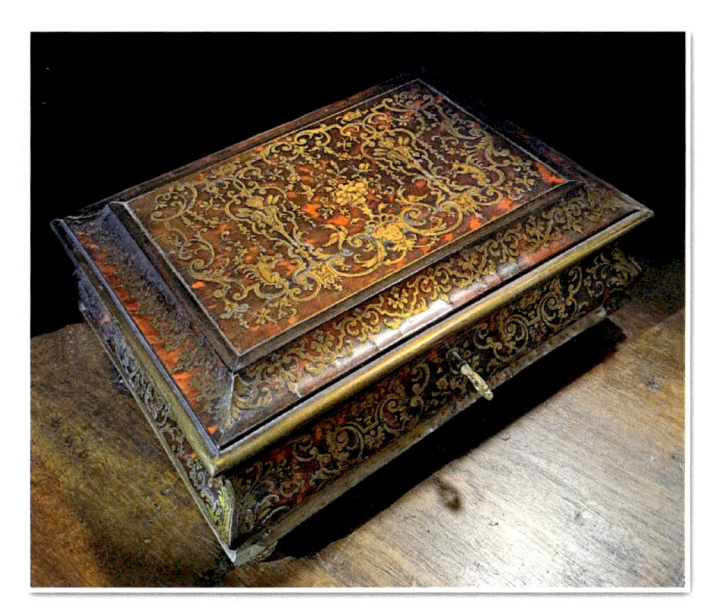

Writing box of rosewood, ebony, tortoiseshell and parcel gilt. Made by Nicolas Sajeot with designs by Jean Bérain the Elder. Paris, France. c.1696

THE TORTOISESHELL BOX
Ink That Echoes Through Time

Writing—the pre-eminent means of communication and the expression of ideas, feelings, and news—allowed certain civilizations to record their existence independently of those who later destroyed them. But civilizations that did not have writing, like the Incas, Aborigines, and tribes of the rainforests, are only known through the study of their artifacts.

In an age of keypads, when cursive writing is no longer taught in American schools, it is interesting to reflect on the many methods and systems devised to record history over the centuries. Even fountain pens, once so familiar to many of us, are now obsolete for practical purposes, and the age of the fine nib dipped into ink is well past. So, it is fascinating to contemplate me—an elaborate, yet straightforward, box with a lock and key. While my exterior suggests that something valuable lies within, nothing gives away my true contents.

Opening me reveals everything necessary to pen a letter. Two inkwells—one for black ink and one for another color—pens, and even sheets of paper. But the lock and its gilded key weren't installed to protect these writing accoutrements. The most valuable items I held were the letters stored beneath the lift-out tray—letters that needed to be kept from prying eyes.

After admiring the decoration on my surface, the next thing people notice is my considerable weight. This is due to the fact that I come from a period before secondary woods were covered with exotic veneers—my foundation is solid rosewood. The term "rosewood" covers over 30 species, but in my case, I am made entirely of Brazilian rosewood (*Dalbergia nigra*). The wood was prized for its rich color, attractive grain, and durability, making it the perfect choice for fine furniture and decorative pieces. My wood is nearly black and often mistaken for ebony.

French ébénistes of the 17th century had access to Brazilian rosewood through trade networks established by European colonial powers. Brazil, a Portuguese colony at the time, was a prominent exporter of rosewood, and its abundance made it highly desirable for luxury furniture production. The dense forests of Brazil provided an ample supply of rosewood, home to indigenous tribes who had little say in how their natural resources were exploited. The tropical woods were shipped to various European countries, including France. While the loss of a few trees had little impact on the Amazon rainforests at the time, today, China's appetite for fine woods is resulting in the stripping of entire forests in Africa, South America, and Southeast Asia. Reports indicate that the Thai government has deployed armed soldiers to protect the last remaining trees.

The French ébénistes also sourced rosewood from India, though this resource was controlled by the English East India Company, who quickly recognized the value of Dalbergia sissoo, known for its beautifully grained heartwood. The tropical climates of these regions provided ideal conditions for the growth of rosewood trees. Throughout the 17th century, factors such as trade routes, political circumstances, and shifts in colonial powers created uncertainty in the supply of exotic timbers. This ensured that rosewood remained highly sought after by French cabinet makers, who used their finest skills to create exquisite furniture and decorative pieces.

To satisfy the sumptuous taste of Louis XIV, my exterior had to be decorated with even more exotic materials. The most favored style of the time was established by André-Charles Boulle, who popularized the use of thin veneers of tortoiseshell in combination with gilded brass and other metals.

André-Charles Boulle (1642–1732), the renowned French cabinetmaker and master of marquetry, achieved great fame during the reigns of Louis XIV, Louis XV, and Louis XVI. His exceptional talent and innovative techniques, particularly his use of tortoiseshell and brass inlay, made him one of history's most celebrated ébénistes. His work exemplified the grandeur and opulence of the French Baroque and Rococo periods. The name "Boulle" has since become synonymous with the distinctive marquetry style he developed, known as "Boulle work" or "Boulle marquetry."

I was made in the workshop of his pupil, Nicolas Sageot, located in the rue du Faubourg-Saint-Antoine. Sageot became a master in 1706 and applied Boulle work to many of the pieces he created. He set up shop near the Bastille prison, which still housed many perceived enemies of the King. Sageot's repertoire included cabinets, bookcases, and commodes. Unfortunately, ill health led to the closure of his workshop in 1720, and in later years, he was declared insane, perhaps haunted by the grotesques that adorned his pieces. He died in an asylum in 1731.

The tortoiseshell work by Sageot and Boulle utilized the shells of the hawksbill sea turtle (Eretmochelys imbricata). These turtles were highly sought after for their distinctive tortoiseshell patterns, making them a prized material for decorative arts and marquetry. The hawksbill turtle has a unique shell pattern characterized by rich amber hues, dark brown or black markings, and a "tortoiseshell" appearance.

Today, the use of hawksbill turtle shells in artistic works, like rosewood, is strictly regulated or prohibited to ensure the preservation of these vulnerable species. The hawksbill sea turtle is listed as critically endangered by the International Union for Conservation of Nature (IUCN) due to threats such as habitat loss, poaching for their shells, and entanglement in fishing gear. Conservation efforts are crucial for their survival and to protect their habitats.

I recall the time when M. Sageot conceived the idea to make me. He had just completed a fine writing desk for an aristocratic family and was waiting for new orders. It was 1696, and Sageot was hard at work building his reputation. At the time, little was created without the design input of Jean Berain. Berain's delightful, whimsical, and symmetrical designs, known as grotesques, were highly influential and used in the decoration of Boulle marquetry, tapestries, textiles, and faience. Berain, the chief designer to the French court, had lodgings near Boulle's in the Louvre.

Berain's influence can be seen in the jolly faces that decorate my top and sides. They are surrounded by flying dragons, fluttering dragonflies, and fairies peeking out of alcoves to gaze upon a compote of fruit, framed by swags of flowers. All these fancies are worked in brass inlays and engraved with shading lines so fine they have never been equaled in later copies. Sageot, not yet a master, didn't stamp his work. You might say the author's identity is inherent in his creations. That practice came a decade later, though even then Sageot didn't consider it necessary.

I was born from the artistic fusion of Jean Berain and Nicolas Sageot, exuding an aura of enchantment. The gargoyles and whimsical figures that adorn my surface invite admirers into a world of imagination. Yesterday, my tortoiseshell glowed with a warm amber hue, and my brass inlay sparkled like stardust. Today, though dimmed with age, my magic endures.
I was acquired as a gift for an important lady in Paris. I recall being delivered through the bustling streets of 17th-century Paris, where the scent of freshly baked bread mingled with the clatter of horse-drawn carriages. Though there were unpleasant street smells, they disappeared as we reached the lady's apartment. Those were the days when I was in constant use. My hinges creaked open and shut daily as letters were written, received, and sometimes hidden within my compartments.

I survived the turbulence of the French Revolution nearly 100 years later. Many luxury items like me were looted or destroyed, but I was fortunate enough to be sent to England, where I awaited a return to France. That return never came, and I had to adapt to new voices. I was considered a curiosity and not required to work, eventually forgotten for another century.

Neglect can be disconcerting. Often, the passage of time and the scars of use are appreciated by collectors, but the most prized of all is an original finish. Though my varnished surface has darkened over the centuries, it was never removed. I retain the same finish as when I left Sageot's shop, and the value this adds is incalculable.

I have had time to reflect on how my sibling writing boxes have served the literate world throughout history. We have seen the apostle Paul pen his letters to the Ephesians, English barons draft the Magna Carta, Shakespeare write his sonnets, and Abraham Lincoln compose the Gettysburg Address. So much of Western civilization was scratched onto paper with ink.

Today, it is understood that a simple writing box was always more than just a utilitarian object. It is a portal to another world, a gateway to inspiration, and a vessel for dreams and aspirations. I was always intended to transcend functionality, and I still do. The letters written with me have witnessed the rise and fall of empires, testifying to love, life, and death. Though I am now retired, I am far from useless. I have lived to see the materials once exploited to create me now respected and protected for a sustainable future. With age comes wisdom and a quiet authority respected by younger generations. If that respect is ever lost, then we will know that civilization has come to an end. While collectors, museums, and historians continue to exist, the spark will be handed on.

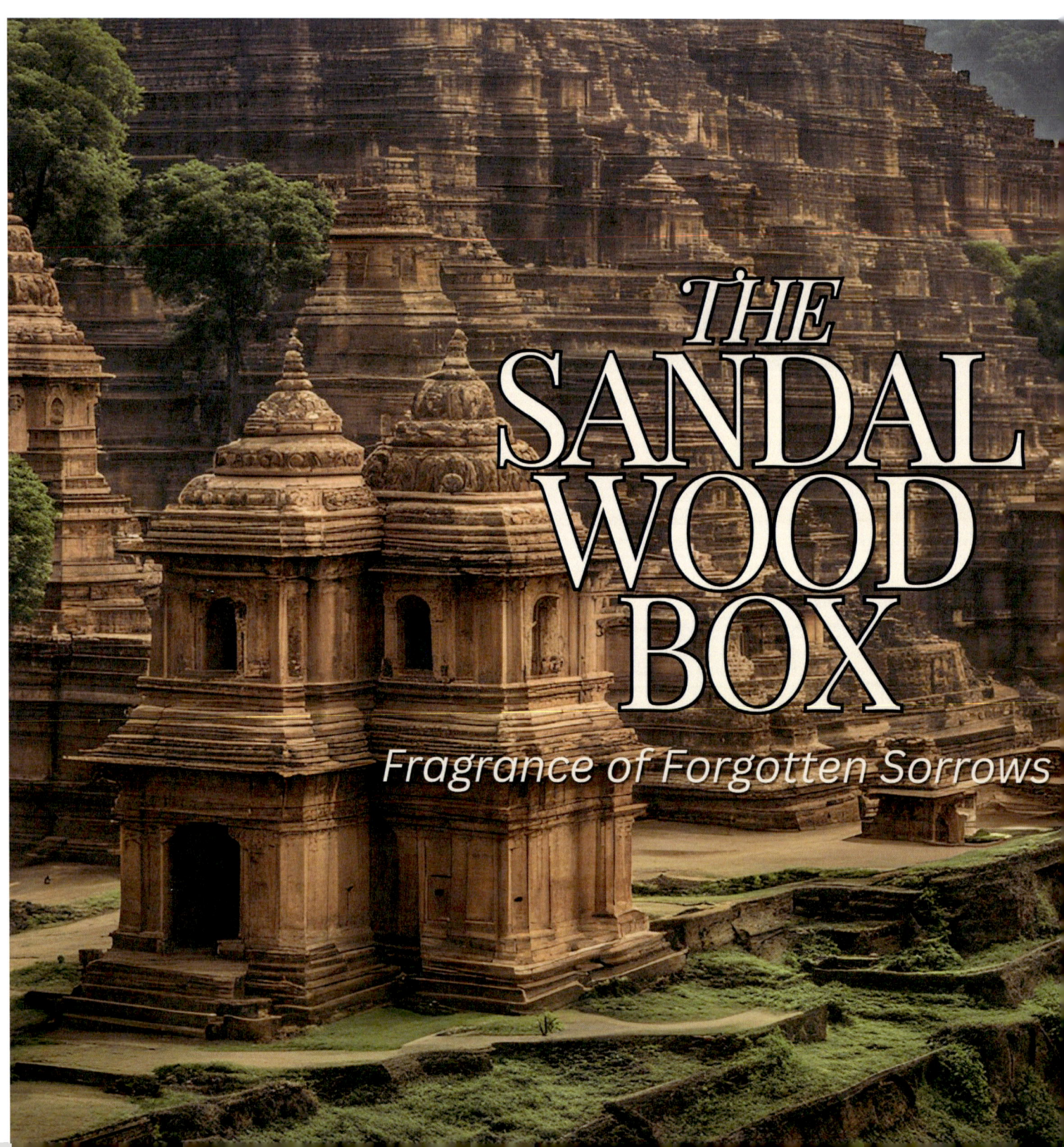

THE SANDAL WOOD BOX

Fragrance of Forgotten Sorrows

THE SANDALWOOD BOX (c. 1849)
Fragrance of Forgotten Sorrows

Jewel casket of solid sandalwood with ebony skirt. Made by Gudigar craftsmen decorated with Hindu deities. Mangalore, Western India. c.1849

THE SANDALWOOD BOX
Fragrance of Forgotten Sorrows

Sandalwood is renowned for its distinct and captivating fragrance, deeply rooted in India. Its scent is warm, rich, and woody, with creamy, slightly sweet undertones. Described as smooth, soothing, and luxurious, it has captivated people worldwide.

In India, sandalwood holds profound cultural and religious significance, used for centuries in rituals, ceremonies, and spiritual practices. The fragrance is considered sacred, believed to have calming and purifying properties, and is commonly used in incense, essential oils, and soaps.

So, it was no surprise when Reverend James Sheridan and his wife, Alice, recognized the distinct aroma of sandalwood as they wandered through the bazaars of Mangalore in 1849. Having recently arrived in Southern India from London, everything felt new and strange. They had been sent by the London Missionary Society (LMS), which established missions throughout India, including regions like Bengal, Madras, Bombay, and South India, where Mangalore is located.

These British missionaries aimed to convert Indians to Christianity and enact social change through education, healthcare, and other philanthropic activities. They sought to establish a British Christian influence in India alongside their religious and social work. Advised that the region was staunchly Hindu and might resist the Mission's activities, the Sheridans approached cautiously, with a "softly, softly" method.

For Alice, the scent of sandalwood was a familiar comfort, reminiscent of home. To the Sheridans, it was almost as though the fragrance had followed them from England. Determined to find its source, they tracked the scent through the market until they stumbled upon a medium-sized workshop where several men sat on the floor, quietly carving intricate objects. I was one of those items nearing completion—a trinket box being crafted by one of the Gudigar Shetty community.

The Gudigars, as they are known, are traditionally associated with sandalwood carving and woodworking. Their expertise has been passed down through generations, and they have played a significant role in the artistic heritage of the region. Today, the art of sandalwood carving is confined to no more than eight families, with a total of about 35 artisans.

The craftsman in charge explained that the quality of sandalwood varies depending on the tree's age, the locality of production, and the part of the tree used. As a rule, the darker the wood, the better the quality. The two boxes being worked on had been commissioned by the East India Company for an exhibition set to take place in Delhi in 1851—one made from lighter wood, the other darker. The East India Company scouts had sought out the best craftsmanship in all disciplines to represent the various regions of imperial India, considered the jewel in the crown of the British Empire. The exhibition wasn't just about displaying Indian artistry but also raising money by acting as a showroom for the world. The scouts knew that for woodwork, and especially sandalwood, the Gudigars of Karnataka were unmatched.

The relationship between Christianity and the Gudigars had been troubled. Forced to leave their ancestral home in Goa by the Portuguese, who demanded conversion to Christianity through violent means, the Gudigars had sought refuge elsewhere. The British, by contrast, took a more pragmatic approach, not insisting on conversion as a condition for successful trade.

Perhaps the Sheridans saw these craftsmen as potential souls to save. The artisans, sensing the need to protect their beliefs, remained guarded. It was Alice who broke the ice by asking about the figures being beautifully carved onto the tops of the boxes. The carvers were happy to explain that these were depictions of gods from their religion. Vishnu, the principal deity, was shown with three faces and four arms. Revered as the preserver and protector of the universe in Hinduism, Vishnu's various avatars, such as Rama and Krishna, are popular subjects in Hindu art and storytelling.

The details were somewhat lost on the Sheridans, as the imagery seemed a little too heathen for their tastes. However, they were intrigued by the figures of two deities holding severed heads and a goddess seated on a serpent. They felt more at ease when the carvers explained that Hindus held a deep connection to the natural world, symbolized by the vines and scrolling foliage that covered every inch of the box. Indeed, no part of a sandalwood box was left untouched by Gudigar craftsmanship.

Despite their differences, the Gudigars and the Sheridans found common ground. Like many who relocate far from home, they all missed familiar comforts, especially food. Alice, who had never adapted well to Indian curries, felt drawn to me, a finely crafted sandalwood box, intending to take me back to England when the time came. This seemed fitting, as my lock and hardware had been made by R. Cooper and Sons of Wolverhampton, England—so in a sense, part of me was returning home.

It was clear that this box was not initially intended for export, as no one other than a Hindu would understand the meaning behind the carvings. I was created for a high-ranking Indian noble, though it was assumed that if purchased by a foreigner at the Great Exhibition, I would leave India. As fate would have it, two years later, the Sheridans, passing through Delhi on their way home, recognized me at the Exhibition and promptly purchased me. Thus, I found myself in the home counties of England.

Sandalwood is botanically identified as Santalum album, and India has been its primary source for centuries. The heartwood of the sandalwood tree is where the fragrance is concentrated, and it can only be harvested after the tree has matured. Because sandalwood is one of the most expensive and sought-after woods in the world, it has been subject to illegal logging and smuggling. To combat this, the government of Mysore, now known as the state of Karnataka in India, has implemented several measures to protect and regulate the harvesting of sandalwood trees. The Sandalwood Act of 1963 contains specific provisions for the protection, conservation, and management of these trees. It establishes regulations for the cultivation, extraction, transportation, and sale of sandalwood. The government also runs awareness campaigns to educate people about the importance of sandalwood conservation, highlighting the ecological significance of these trees and the need to protect them for future generations.

And so, two years elapsed between the Sheridans witnessing my creation in the Mangalore workshop and finally purchasing me in New Delhi. I was made of darker sandalwood, meriting finer workmanship, and ensuring that my fragrance would endure longer. My master carved my decorations over many weeks, using chisels of ever-decreasing size, making the finest details nearly imperceptible to the human eye.

While I enjoyed peaceful oblivion in a china cabinet for 100 years in southern England, my lighter-skinned brother was acquired for display in The Museum of Art at Marlborough House, a historic art museum in London, now known as the Victoria and Albert Museum. Sir John Charles Robinson, a prominent art historian and the museum's curator, wrote a famous book in 1859 titled *The Treasury of Ornamental Art*, in which he remarked on the craftsmanship of my brother box:

"In the present example, the decoration is admirably subordinated to the leading lines and members of the composition. Even the three Hindu deities, and the arcades in the center panel, being so conventional in their treatment, appear to blend sensibly into the surrounding floral ornaments."

But his celebrity didn't last long. Soon, my brother box was confined to storage and replaced by younger, more fascinating exhibits, while I remained loved and cherished in the warm, moist atmosphere of the British coastal town of Eastbourne. On quiet nights, I could hear the crashing waves, reminding me of my birthplace lifetimes ago.

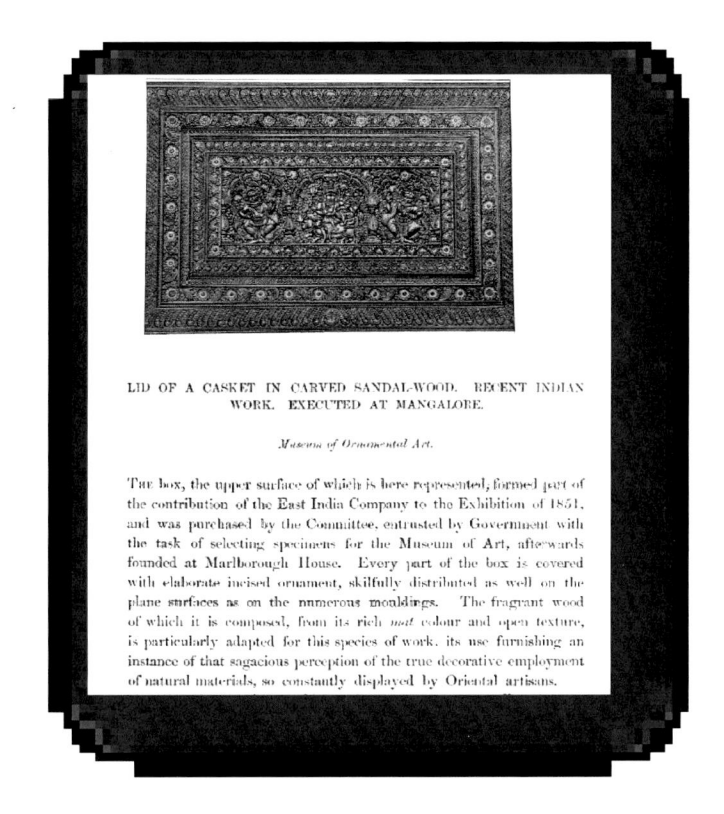

LID OF A CASKET IN CARVED SANDAL-WOOD. RECENT INDIAN WORK. EXECUTED AT MANGALORE.

Museum of Ornamental Art.

THE box, the upper surface of which is here represented, formed part of the contribution of the East India Company to the Exhibition of 1851, and was purchased by the Committee, entrusted by Government with the task of selecting specimens for the Museum of Art, afterwards founded at Marlborough House. Every part of the box is covered with elaborate incised ornament, skilfully distributed as well on the plane surfaces as on the numerous mouldings. The fragrant wood of which it is composed, from its rich *nut* colour and open texture, is particularly adapted for this species of work, its use furnishing an instance of that sagacious perception of the true decorative employment of natural materials, so constantly displayed by Oriental artisans.

Fame is fleeting. My brother box is now lost to posterity, and the Sheridans lie buried in the churchyard where Reverend Sheridan preached for so many years. The younger generation of Gudigars has created a website (gudigars.com) to celebrate their community and skills, though the elder generation, who continue their carvings, have little use for it.

I now live in America, and my story rests on these pages. It isn't always the swiftest that wins the race—sometimes, late flowerings are the sweetest.

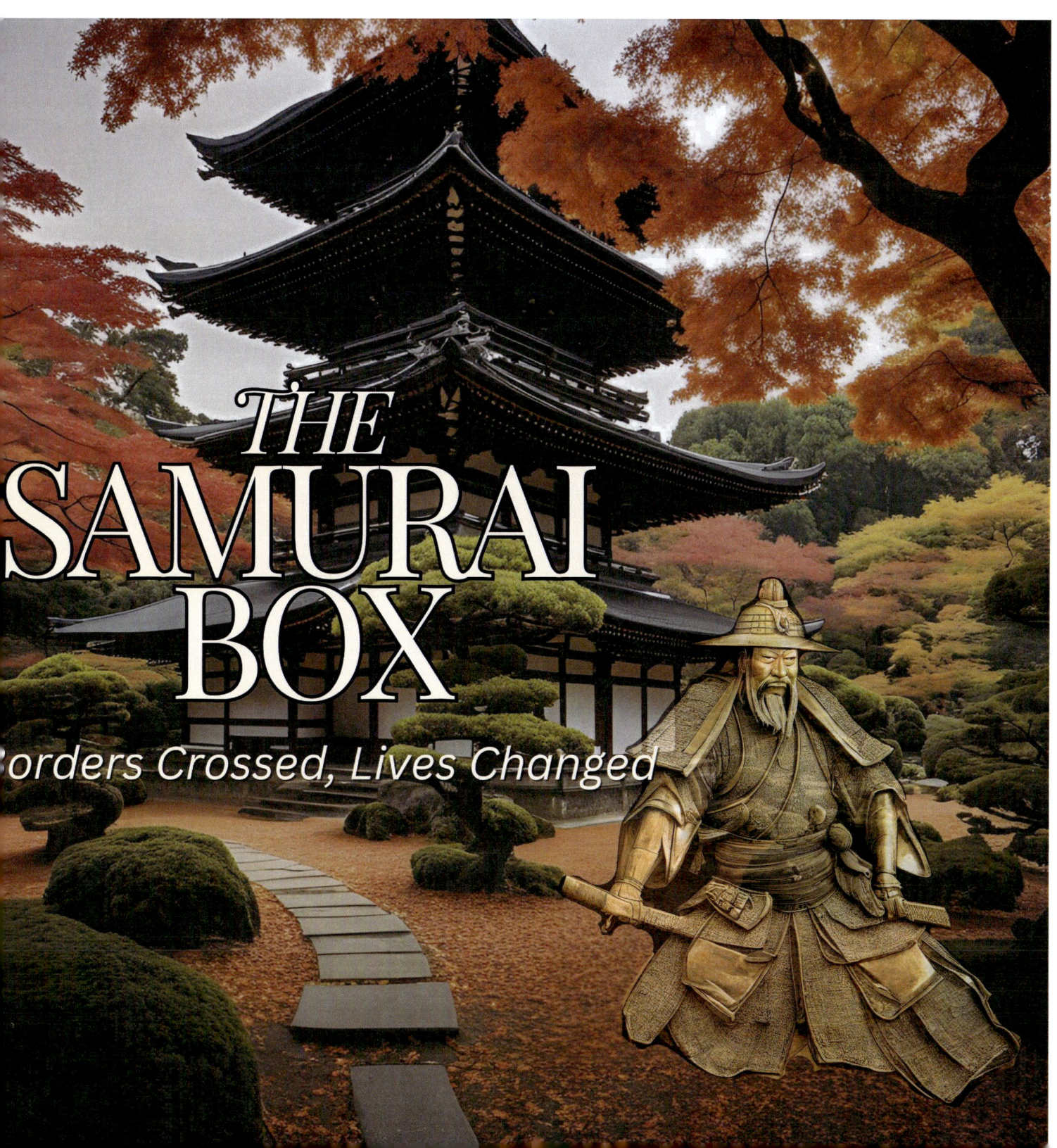

THE SAMURAI BOX

Borders Crossed, Lives Changed

THE SAMURAI BOX (c. 1830)
Borders Crossed, Lives Changed

Presentation gift box of Paulownia wood. Made by Japanese Edo craftsmen decorated with gofun chrysanthemums. Tokyo, Japan, c.1830.

THE SAMURAI BOX C.1830
Borders Crossed, Lives Changed

I am a recent immigrant to the USA, having arrived directly from Tokyo, Japan, in May 2020— just before the world shut down due to Covid. But the trees that provided the wood for me made their journey nearly 200 years earlier.

This is a story about migration and why we shouldn't judge based on first impressions. Appearances can be deceptive, and never more so than in my case. At first glance, the wood I'm made from appears ordinary. I am constructed from Paulownia wood—the fast-growing, lightweight, and unremarkable "plain Jane" of the timber world. But look more closely at the exquisite craftsmanship in my simple lines. Notice how my surface is adorned with white chrysanthemums, symbols of immortality and perfect health in Japan. These aren't painted on, but made from Gofun.

Gofun is a traditional Japanese decorative technique using finely powdered oyster shells mixed with a binder, usually glue, to create intricate designs. The paste is applied to the surface and shaped using various tools. This technique has been highly regarded for centuries, showcasing Japanese artistry.

These chrysanthemums—symbols of the Imperial Chrysanthemum Throne—along with the dark, aged color of my wood, attest to my considerable age.

I was created during the Edo period (1603–1867), a time when Japan was ruled by the Tokugawa shogunate and its 300 regional daimyo, or feudal lords.

The daimyo were powerful territorial lords who held significant political and military authority. They governed their respective domains with extensive control over taxation, justice, and their own armies of samurai warriors. Their power was granted in exchange for loyalty and military service to the shogunate.

In 1830, I was commissioned as a gift from Tokugawa Nariaki—also known as Mito Nariaki, a daimyo with impeccable taste and a prominent political figure in Japan. Nariaki, known for his outspoken views, gifted me to the commander of his samurai army in recognition of a job well done.

While the gift itself has long been forgotten, I remain as a testament to its importance.

The Paulownia tree, from which I was made, is considered sacred in Japan, symbolizing prosperity, longevity, and good fortune. It has been valued for centuries, used in temples, shrines, and aristocratic residences. While not as visually dramatic as some other woods, its light golden hue and straight grain pattern lend it an elegant simplicity.

Paulownia wood is lightweight yet strong, making it easy to work with, while its natural resistance to decay and pests enhances its durability. Even after 260 years, I remain intact, with no cracks, and my lid still slides off as smoothly as it did the day I was made. The wood's insulating properties also give it high fire resistance, with an ignition temperature of around 400°C—nearly twice that of other woods.

In Japan, I am known as Kiri (桐) wood. By coincidence, the trees that produce Kiri wood began their journey to Pennsylvania, USA, in the same year I was made—1830. At that time, Japan was closed to foreigners, but a German doctor named Philip Franz von Siebold, working for the Dutch military, managed to send thousands of plants back to Europe, including the Paulownia tree.

By the 1840s, the Paulownia tree had taken root in America, where it thrived. It became known for its rapid growth—adding up to 15 feet per year—and its ability to survive in harsh conditions. Over time, it became a symbol of resilience, surviving wildfires and regenerating quickly from its roots.

Paulownia trees have cultural significance in Japan. It's customary to plant a Paulownia tree when a daughter is born, so that by the time she is ready to marry, the tree can be harvested and made into a dresser as a wedding gift.

In modern times, Paulownia trees have been suggested for carbon capture projects due to their ability to absorb carbon dioxide, making them a sustainable choice for timber. In addition, the wood has become commercially valuable, fetching between $10 and $15 per board foot. This value led to the infamous "Fairmount Park Chainsaw Massacre" in the 1980s, when thieves cut down Paulownia trees in Philadelphia to sell the wood back to Japan.

Paulownia's fast growth, natural resistance to pests, and ability to thrive in poor conditions have made it a favorite for sustainable forestry. Its large leaves absorb pollutants, and its wood has become valuable both commercially and environmentally.

In May 2020, as the Covid-19 pandemic took hold, I completed my journey from Tokyo to Pennsylvania. Like my tree ancestors, I entered a nation of immigrants at a time of great turbulence. Yet, like them, I have found a new home, where I am appreciated. Though Japanese immigrants were once interned following the bombing of Pearl Harbor, the story has a sweet ending. Today, the purple flowers of the Paulownia tree are beloved by American bees, producing top-quality honey.

We immigrants always strive to give back more than we take, as a gesture of our gratitude for being welcomed into new lands.

THE BIBLICAL BOX

Cleopatra's Secret Treasure

THE BIBLICAL BOX (c. 1990)
Cleopatra's Secret Treasure

Table box for trinkets of Thuya burl wood. Made by traditional woodworkers and finished withhand rubbed shellac. Essaouira, Morocco, c.1990.

THE BIBLICAL BOX
Cleopatra's Secret Treasure

No one seeing me now could possibly imagine my transition from darkness into light—a journey spanning 200 years. I've emerged from centuries of underground obscurity into the blinding light of day, finally appreciated by many. It's an improbable story, for I am the most exotic creation in the world that nobody has heard of.

My history is a long one. I am even mentioned in the Bible. I have been used since the days of Solomon and David, when I was called "thyine wood." I was referenced by John in the Book of Revelation and also in the First Book of Kings, Chapter 10, as part of the treasures brought to Solomon by the navy of Hiram. The Greeks called me Thuya, meaning "sacrifice," because they used my oil as incense in their religious ceremonies.

I am Thuya wood (pronounced twee-ah), not to be confused with *Thuja plicata*, which is found in the Pacific Northwest of North America and commonly known as Western Red Cedar. No, that wood is straight-grained, practical, but unremarkable. I am Thuya wood, derived from the *Tetraclinis articulata* tree, native only to the Atlas Mountains of Morocco. I have been here since the Phoenicians brought me in 1200 BC and have never left.

Unlike the tall red cedar, which produces long planks, I am known for my burls, which are as beautiful as they are fragrant. The Greeks and Romans prized my burls, competing for furniture made from them. In ancient times, two great ambitions drove powerful men: to become a dictator and to own a table made from Thuya Burl—known as citron wood or thyine to the Romans. It is said that Cicero's wife owned a thyine burl table worth what would be fifty thousand dollars today. Cleopatra herself favored me.

I am also one of the most misunderstood and misidentified woods. People often call me burl walnut, bird's eye maple, or amboyna because of the striking "eyes" that dot my surface. These eyes are the rootlets of small branches that formed underground. But my beauty is more than these eyes—it lies in the swirls and eddies on my surface that reflect life itself. Calm waters and turbulent whirls mark the passage of time, just as my markings formed in an environment that never saw the light of day.

Most burls form on tree trunks, but my burl developed underground in the rootstock. Because of the rich oils I contain, I survived long after my parent tree died. In the Atlas Mountains, where Thuya trees, cedars, and oaks once stood tall, centuries of overharvesting and forest fires have left vast areas treeless. Yet, it is in these cleared areas that burls like mine are discovered. Often, there is no trace of the tree left above ground, and these burls—like truffles—must be unearthed by chance.

My personal history began that way. Some burls are carefully harvested from the roots of the Thuya tree, requiring the earth to be dug away from the base of the tree without causing damage. Finding these burls is no easy task, as they are small and lack a stump to guide searchers. I was discovered by random digging and, caked in clay and stones, transported down the mountain by donkey. At the time, I revealed nothing of the glory I would become.

In Morocco, particularly in the city of Essaouira, Thuya woodcraft has a long-standing tradition. Artisans have been working with Thuya wood for centuries, creating handmade items such as decorative boxes, chess sets, and carved trays. Thuya wood is highly prized for its unique grain patterns and rich, warm colors, ranging from deep red to golden brown. The craft industry is an essential part of the local economy, showcasing the skill passed down through generations of Moroccan artisans.

The figured Thuya wood primarily comes from the burl formations found in the roots of the *Tetraclinis articulata* tree. The intricate patterns and colors make it highly desirable for decorative woodworking. France, as the colonial power, began exporting Thuya in the 1830s, and their cabinetmakers were the first to use its exotic veneers for furniture in the grandest chateaux and city palaces. By the 1850s, Thuya had made its way to England, with royal cabinetmakers like Holland & Sons incorporating it into their fine English craftsmanship.

In Morocco, the craft of working with solid Thuya wood has been passed down through generations, preserving traditional techniques and designs that have evolved over centuries. Today, this craft remains an important cultural heritage and a thriving industry. The natural hand-rubbed shellac finish highlights the enduring beauty of Thuya wood, while the wood's distinctive fragrance adds to its appeal.

When freshly cut or sanded, Thuya wood releases a strong aromatic scent, described as a mix between cedar and sandalwood. This scent, attributed to aromatic oils within the wood, adds to its desirability and contributes to its resistance to decay and insects. Thuya wood products retain this fragrance long after they are crafted, creating a sensory experience that enhances the appeal of owning and handling such pieces.

Thuya wood has long been important to the economy of Essaouira, a port city that has now been declared a UNESCO World Heritage site. The craft industry surrounding Thuya wood has created a demand for decorative items and souvenirs, attracting tourists and collectors from around the world. The industry supports local artisans and provides income for their families, helping sustain livelihoods in the community. I was purchased on eBay and exported from Essaouira to the USA as part of a Moroccan government-controlled program that promotes prosperity while ensuring sustainable practices. Every time a tree is harvested for its wood, another is planted in its place.

As the burl root is freed from night's hold, Essaouira finally welcomes a bright dawn.

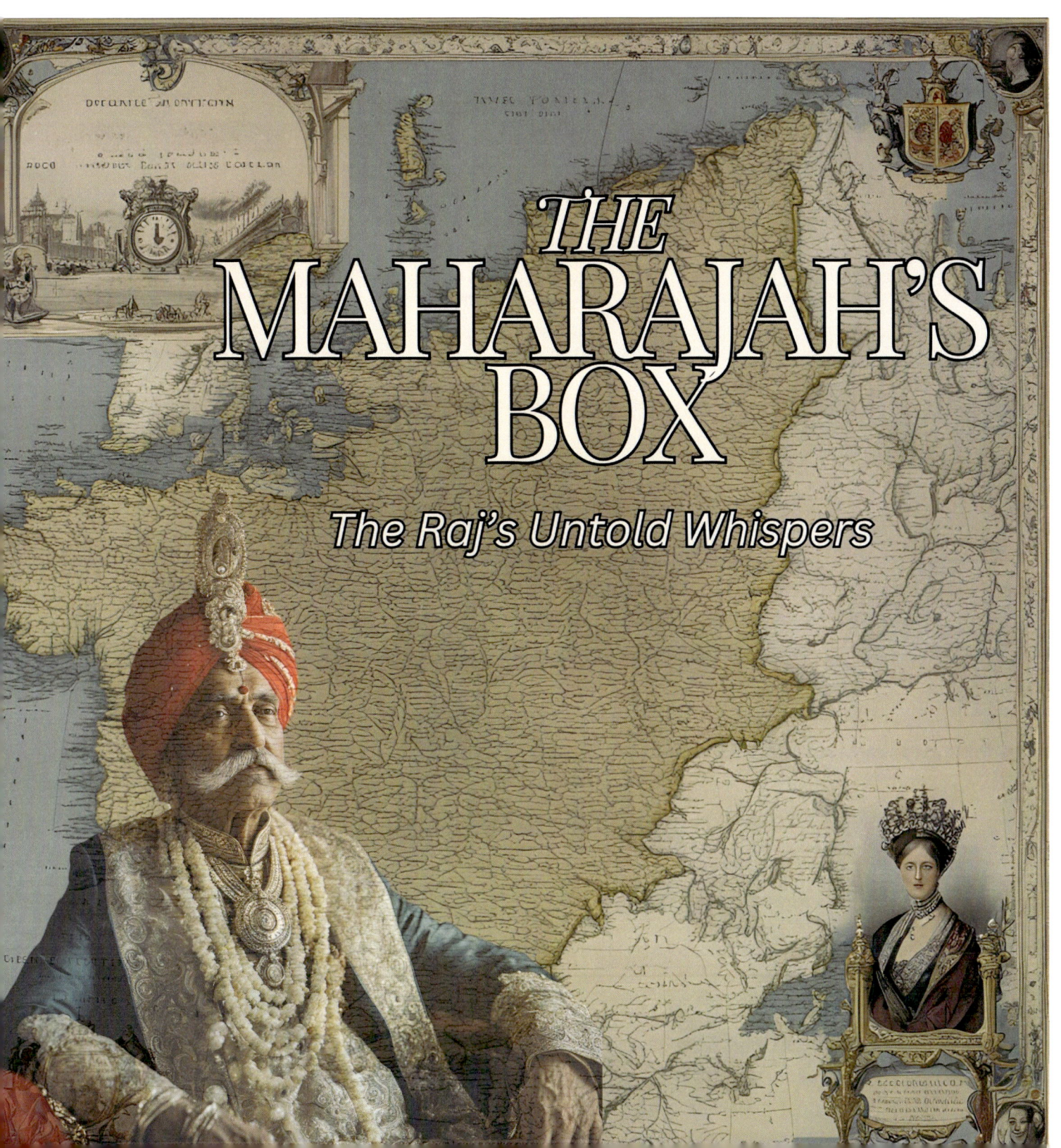

THE MAHARAJAH'S BOX

The Raj's Untold Whispers

THE MARAJA'S BOX (c. 1849)
The Raj's Untold Whispers.

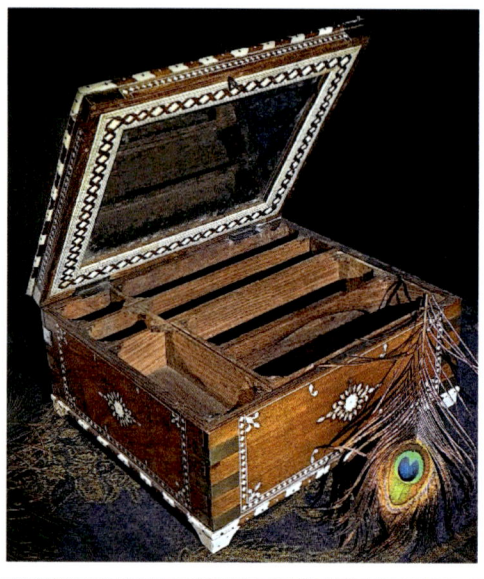

Presentation casket of Indian rosewood decorated with ivory and ebony. Made in the workshop of Maharaja Hira Singh to his design. Hoshiarpur, Punjab, Pakistan. c.1849.

THE MAHARAJA'S BOX
The Raj's Untold Whispers

The Maharaja of Hoshiarpur, His Highness Colonel Maharaja Hira Singh, or to give him his full grandiose title: Colonel H.H. Farzand-i-Arjumand, Aqidat-Paiwand-i-Daulat-i-Inglishia, Baarar Bans Sarmur, Raja-i-Rajagan, Maharaja Shri Sir Hira Singh Malvendra Bahadur, Maharaja of Nabha, GCSI, GCIE, was a great friend of Britain. These titles—GCSI, Grand Commander of the Order of the Star of India, and GCIE, Grand Commander of the Order of the Indian Empire—were honors bestowed during British colonial rule for significant contributions to the Empire.

In 1878, Hira Singh sent a contingent of 700 soldiers to fight alongside the British in Afghanistan, earning him great favor with the Deputy Commissioner. (Yes, the British were fighting in Afghanistan a century before the Russians or Americans). Major Morrison, the Deputy Commissioner, introduced the Maharaja to British literature, particularly novels and poetry.

When Queen Victoria's Golden Jubilee approached in 1887, the Maharaja sought to present her with a special gift, something deeply personal and detailed, as he was known for being a micromanager. He decided that the gift would be a casket, handcrafted by the finest local artisans, blending the aesthetics and culture of Punjab with clear British influences.

The box would be made of the finest Indian Rosewood. Given that two species share the name "Indian Rosewood," he specified the slow-growing *Dalbergia latifolia* from the foothills of the Himalayas, rather than the more common *Dalbergia sissoo*, which, while useful, was unworthy of a royal gift. *D. latifolia* has heartwood in shades of light golden brown to deep purple with dark streaks and a dense, fragrant quality that made it highly prized and difficult to work with.

Today, D. latifolia is protected under Indian law and listed in Appendix II of the Convention on International Trade in Endangered Species (CITES), ensuring its conservation through sustainable forest management.

In addition to the rosewood base, the Maharaja insisted that the casket's visible surfaces be adorned with the finest African ivory from Bombay, known for its bluish-white sheen. The more common Indian ivory, which is duller and opaque, would not suffice for a royal gift. The ivory would be pegged carefully to prevent it from coming loose.

Furthermore, the Maharaja wanted the casket's internal drawers to display some of the creamy-white sapwood from the *Dalbergia latifolia* tree, a feature that highlighted the use of only the finest materials. The inside of the lid would be adorned with a beveled mirror, crafted by Ganga Ram, an artisan known for his mastery of such work.

Being familiar with British military traditions, the Maharaja also requested that the casket have metal inset corner mounts, reminiscent of English campaign furniture.

Work on the casket began in 1885, leaving ample time for its transportation to England, as Queen Victoria was not expected to travel to India to receive tributes. The initial phase involved creating a working prototype, or "mock-up," to address any design issues before final production. This version was made from less expensive Sheesham wood, and the ivory inlay was not pegged, as it would be on the final piece. The prototype was lighter and smaller, without the mirror or feet, and served to avoid last-minute surprises.

His Highness made only minor adjustments to the prototype, the most significant being related to the ivory inlay. The artisans had covered much of the box with ivory, but the Maharaja, with his instinctive understanding of the 80/20 rule—decades before it became widely known—ordered that only 20% of the box's surface should feature ivory, allowing the beauty of the wood to dominate.

Upon completion, the casket was presented to the Maharaja for approval. Satisfied, he returned it to the workshop for careful packing and shipment to England. However, as fate would have it, a mix-up occurred. The prototype was sent to Queen Victoria instead of the original.

Years later, as the workshop was being remodeled, the original casket was found. Realizing the error, the workshop owner, Karm Chand Ganga Ram, chose to inform the Maharaja himself—a risky move, given the circumstances. In another era, such a mistake might have cost Ganga Ram his life, but the Maharaja graciously accepted both the apology and the casket.

One evening, while entertaining a British friend, the Maharaja shared the story in confidence and gifted the casket to him, on the condition that the mix-up never be revealed. The friend returned to his home in Thornton Heath, Surrey, England, keeping his word. Eventually, the casket presented to Queen Victoria was given to the Victoria and Albert Museum, where it was praised as a fine example of Anglo-Indian craftsmanship.

Years later, the British friend fondly recalled the Maharaja's favorite poem, quoting in a Scottish accent:
"The best laid schemes o' Mice an' Men, Gang aft agley. An' lea'e us nought but grief an' pain,
For promis'd joy!"
—Robert Burns, 1785
Burns' poem reflected on the plight of a mouse whose home was destroyed by a plow—a poignant metaphor for the way history, driven by empires, often plows through people and places. Little did they know that less than 60 years later, the partition of India would divide the Maharaja's beloved homeland at the cost of over a million lives.

During the partition of India in 1947, regions like Hoshiarpur experienced communal violence and mass migrations, as Punjab was divided between India and Pakistan. The religious partition led to immense suffering and displacement, and the scars of that period still influence the region today.

While the rosewood trees and the people of India are slowly recovering, I continue to keep my secrets—but now in America.

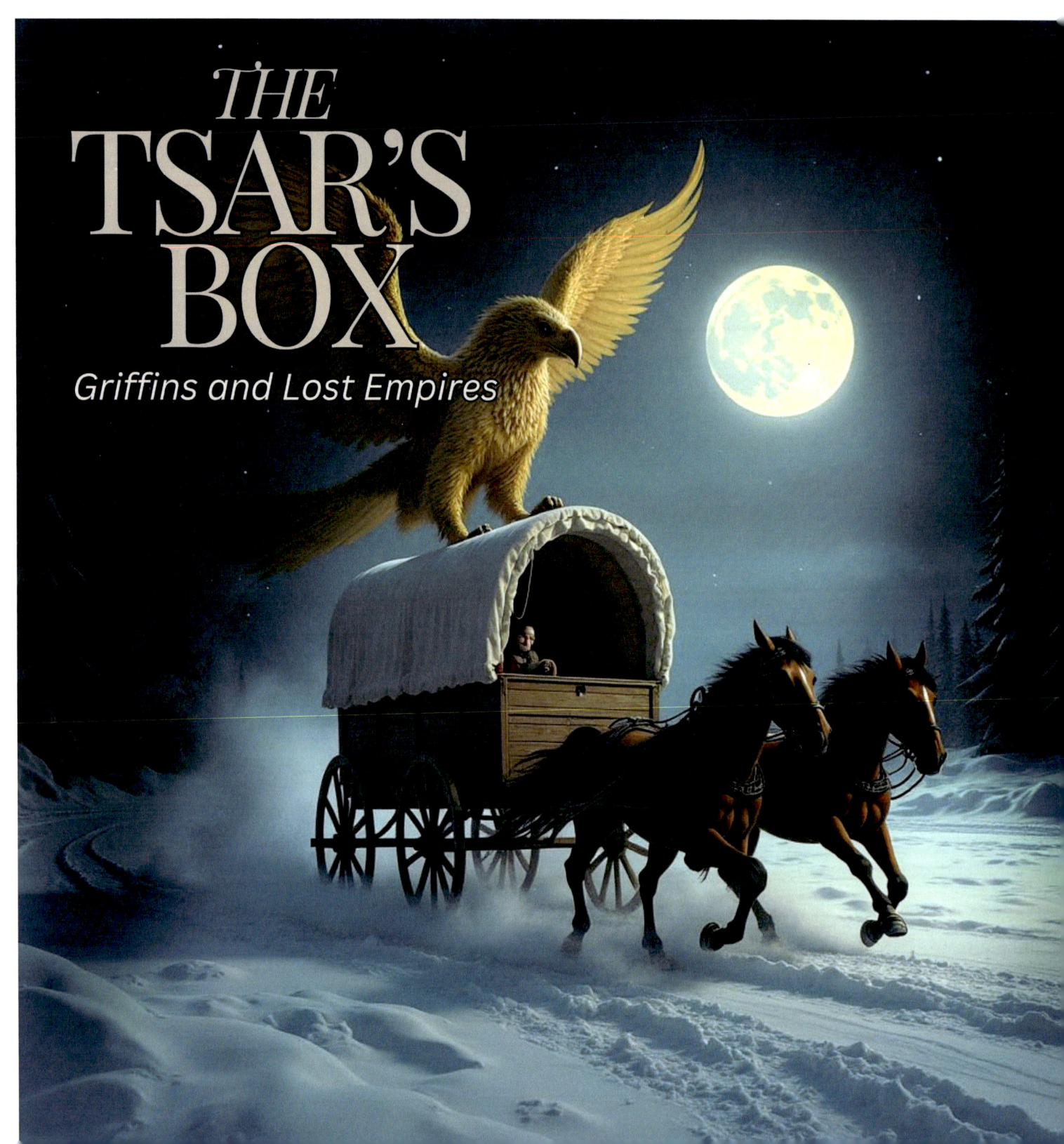

THE TSAR'S BOX

Griffins and Lost Empires

THE TSAR'S BOX (c. 1890)
Griffins and Lost Empires

Jewel box of Karelian birch adorned with silver fittings. Made in St Petersburg for General Alexei Brusilov as gift for his wife. c. 1890

THE TSAR'S BOX
Griffins and Lost Empires

Karelian birch is sometimes referred to as "masur" birch due to its association with the Masurian region in northeastern Poland. The term "masur" originates from Masuria, a historical region in Poland and western Russia. To most residents of Hungerford, Miss Lavender was a sweet little old lady who made twice- weekly visits to the grocery store. Few knew of her extraordinary past as a young governess in Saint Petersburg, Russia. At just 18 years old, she had traveled to become the English governess to the children of General Alexei Brusilov, a distinguished officer in the Tsar's cavalry. Little did she know that she was more of a status symbol than a serious educator; the children already spoke English and French fluently, as the Russian aristocracy considered Russian a language of the lower classes, while the upper class preferred French for conversation.

For our story, it is essential to understand the Romanov family's love for Karelian birch. The last imperial dynasty of Russia had a particular fondness for this rare wood. Tsar Nicholas II and his family commissioned furniture, decorative panels, and intricate woodwork made from Karelian birch for their palaces, including the Winter Palace in St. Petersburg and the Alexander Palace in Tsarskoye Selo. Their personal items often featured this unique and luxurious wood, including jewelry boxes similar to me. The Romanovs' admiration for Karelian birch solidified its reputation in the world of fine craftsmanship.

This splendor ended tragically when Tsar Nicholas II and his family were executed by the Bolsheviks during the Russian Civil War on the night of July 16-17, 1918. Following the abdication of Nicholas II in 1917, the Romanovs were held under house arrest before being transferred to the Ipatiev House in Yekaterinburg. There, in the early hours of July 17, they were executed by a firing squad on the orders of local Soviet authorities. Their brutal execution marked the end of the Romanov dynasty and set in motion the escape of Miss Lavender and the family of the Russian officer she served.

Many aristocrats, members of the nobility, and others associated with the former imperial regime were persecuted or faced the confiscation of their properties. Fleeing Russia became the only option for survival. General Brusilov chose to remain behind, but for his family, he arranged an escape route across Russia to the eastern port of Vladivostok. Our journey began, spanning over a month through a disrupted Trans-Siberian Railway system, with constant stops for troop movements. At times, we traveled by carriage or cart, sleeping during the day and moving at night to avoid detection.

During this perilous journey, my contents of family jewels and gold coins were kept secure by my little gold key. Hidden in an old sack, I traveled unnoticed, protecting the family's last remnants of wealth. The journey was exhausting and dangerous, but far more challenging for an English girl barely into adulthood, like Miss Lavender.

By the end of the journey, little was left of the family's treasures. When they finally reached Vladivostok, General Brusilov's wife could only reward Miss Lavender with the box that once held the jewels. I am that box. Though Miss Lavender initially thought me to be made of inferior wood, I am crafted from the same Karelian birch so loved by the Romanovs.

Unlike European-made boxes, where a single block of wood is cut to separate the body and lid, my lid and body were made separately. My edges and joints are concealed by veneers, likely due to the difficulty of working with Karelian birch, which is not available in large pieces. This wood, prized for its unique figuring, became popular in the 19th century, particularly in Russia. Karelian birch, with its rare burl formations and swirling patterns, is specific to the Karelia region, immortalized by Sibelius in his *Karelia Suite*.

Karelian birch is challenging to work with due to its irregular grain and unique figuring. It requires sharp tools and careful attention to achieve clean cuts, but skilled craftsmen appreciate its beauty despite the difficulties.
In my case, my silver attachments feature winged griffins, creatures of significance in Russian culture and folklore. Griffins—beasts with the body of a lion and the wings of an eagle—symbolize power, protection, and guardianship. In Russian mythology, they are seen as guardians of treasures, defending sacred sites and important places. Their wings symbolize transcendence, the ability to connect the earthly and the divine.

These griffins, decorating me, are the protectors of the box, though the family treasures have long since disappeared. They continue to guard what remains: the precious Karelian birch from which I am made. They embody the protective forces that watched over Miss Lavender and the family during their escape, just as I protected the jewels within.

One can ask no more from them.

Just as I protected the jewels, Miss Lavender protected the family, and the griffins protected the box. So too, must each of us protect something valuable on this mysterious journey we call life.

"So long lives this
And this gives life to thee."
—William Shakespeare, *Sonnet 18*

THE NOMAD'S BOX

The Silent Diplomat

THE NOMAD'S BOX (c. 1970)
Out of Africa, Into History

Accessory box of African blackwood decorated with German silver. Made by nomadic Tuareg craftsman for sale in Bamako. Timbuktu, Republic of Mali, West Africa. c.1970.

THE NOMAD'S BOX
Out of Africa, Into History

If the whereabouts of Mauritania and the Federation of Mali are unfamiliar to you, or if the recent history of the Tuareg peoples of the Western Sahara is obscure, let me enlighten you.

The Mali Empire was a grand and influential power in West Africa during the 13th to 17th centuries. Founded by Sundiata Keita in the 13th century, it rose to become one of the wealthiest empires in African history, known for its vast territory that included parts of modern-day Mali, Senegal, Gambia, Guinea, Niger, Burkina Faso, and Mauritania. Its capital, Niani, was a hub of trade, scholarship, and Islamic culture. The empire thrived due to its control over key trans-Saharan trade routes, particularly in gold and salt, which brought immense wealth and allowed for impressive urban and architectural development.

Under the leadership of Mansa Musa (1312–1337 AD), often regarded as one of the wealthiest individuals in history, the Mali Empire reached its zenith. Mansa Musa's pilgrimage to Mecca in the 14th century showcased the empire's vast wealth to the world. The Mali Empire left a lasting cultural legacy, with iconic sites such as the Great Mosque of Djenné and the University of Sankore in Timbuktu, both of which are recognized as UNESCO World Heritage sites. However, its influence began to decline with the arrival of the Portuguese, who opened sea trade routes around West Africa.
When empires meet, ambassadors emerge—not always appointed by governments, but by their cultures. These ambassadors are travelers and communicators, representing their nations, ideologies, and heritage with clarity and conviction. They need to be resilient, able to traverse challenging terrains and situations. I, too, was born to be such an ambassador.

I was created to represent the pride and history of the Tuareg people, nomads of the Western Sahara, who lived their lives traversing shifting sands. These enigmatic people established centers of learning like Timbuktu and built magnificent religious monuments like the Great Mosque of Djenné. As nomads, they moved constantly, riding camels across hot desert expanses. Although I do not have legs, it was always understood that I would journey across time and space with human hands guiding me. My travels, though, would be harsh, so I was crafted from one of the toughest woods—African blackwood—and adorned with silver.

In the days of the Mali Empire, I would have been adorned in gold. Mansa Musa's wealth was legendary, with gold flowing through his kingdom like water. But by the 1970s, only silver remained, and even that was frequently alloyed. Still, I was built to proclaim my message like a billboard—my bold, masculine central panels balanced by delicate, feminine edges, a silver moon floating in an infinite dark sky. Oddly enough, my wood has become more valuable than my silver; African blackwood is now one of the most precious woods in the world.

African blackwood, also known as Mozambique ebony (*Dalbergia melanoxylon*), is a small tree native to Sub-Saharan West Africa, including Mali. Its dark, dense heartwood has been sought after for over 5,000 years, used in fine woodworking, musical instruments, and ornamental carvings. It's said that even young King Tutankhamen sat on a chair made from this wood.

The wood is incredibly valuable, and poachers now harvest young trees, only 2-3 inches in diameter, resulting in narrow planks suitable for small items like me. African blackwood is now the most expensive wood in the world, valued at several times the price of sandalwood. Though often called 'ebony,' it's not related to true ebony, another highly prized black wood.

Humans have an innate urge to travel, to seek something beyond the present. We look for our gods in the places we've yet to visit, but as we conquer one horizon after another, even the skies no longer seem so mysterious. We've learned how to fly, and yet no passenger on a commercial flight has ever reported spotting a bearded old man in the clouds, surrounded by angels. Still, it's hard to prove a negative, so we keep an open mind.

Gordon (Gordie) Williams, a CIA field officer, was assigned to West Africa in the 1970s. Affiliated with the American Embassy in Mali, his job was to travel the vast country, keeping tabs on the political climate since Mali's independence from France in 1960. Mali is three times the size of Germany and twice the area of Texas, so this was no small task. While there was political discontent in some quarters, there was also a resurgence of national pride through the arts and crafts of the past.

Gordie spent much of his time in Timbuktu, a city founded by the Tuareg people around 1100 AD. The Tuareg, known for their distinctive indigo-blue clothing, were semi-nomadic and lived across the Saharan regions of North Africa. Blue had long been a symbol of Tuareg identity, indicating wealth and status within their society.

It was in a Tuareg tent in Timbuktu that Gordie spotted me, just before I was due to be shipped to a tourist shop in Bamako. The Tuareg artisans, masters of metalwork and woodcraft, had created me with intricate designs of ebony and silver. My six silver panels were hand-cut and inset into carefully chiseled ebony, then decorated with a small sharp chisel in a rapid rocking motion. No dovetail joints here, just a simple, sturdy construction, crafted without modern tools, all of it easily packed away on the back of a camel.

By establishing a cordial rapport with my Tuareg maker, Hassan, Gordie was able to understand the pulse of the region, feeling out opportunities and threats to American interests. I, meanwhile, continued my role as an ambassador, carrying the spirit of the Tuareg with me.

Gordie eventually returned to Washington, D.C., bringing me as a gift for his wife. She delighted in my unique appearance and passed on my story to her friends. But my existence was nearly threatened in the late 1970s when the Hunt brothers, Nelson and William, tried to corner the global silver market. Their efforts drove silver prices to record highs, and many silver antiques were melted down for scrap. Luckily, I survived. Ironically, while my silver panels are worth little today, my ebony wood has become priceless.

Ambassadors know which parts of history to highlight and which to gloss over. The Tuareg people once traded gold, salt, and ivory, but they also traded slaves—mostly Bella tribesmen from Niger and Mali, who still live in semi-slavery under the Tuareg today. It's a story that both continents— Africa and America—prefer to ignore.

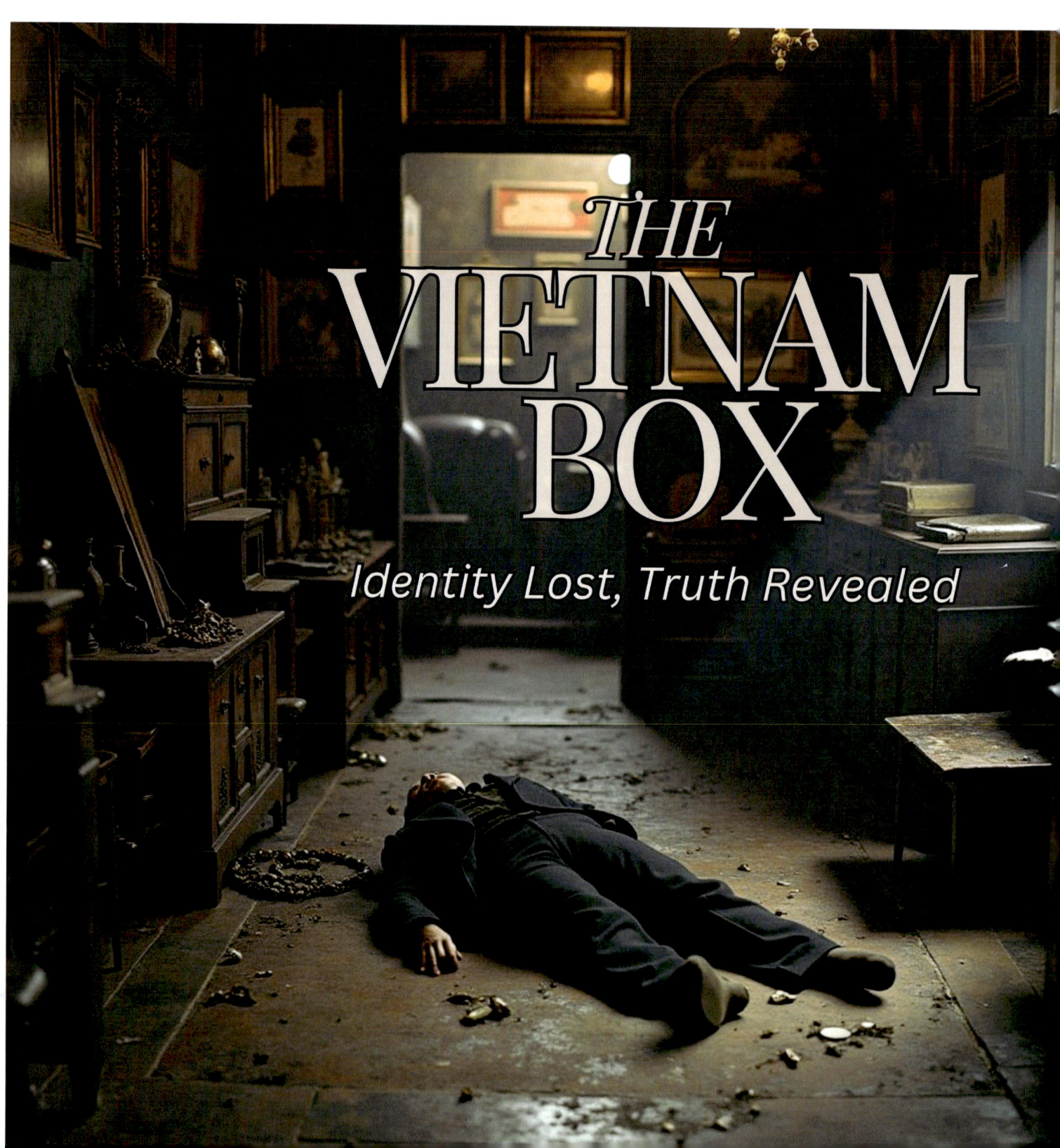

THE VIETNAM BOX

Identity Lost, Truth Revealed

THE VIETNAM BOX (c. 1820)
Identity Lost, Truth Revealed

Trinket box made of Siamese rosewood inlaid with mother of pearl and an ivory knop. Made by traditional craftsmen for the royal palace in Hue. Chuong Ngo village, Hanoi (formerly Tonkin), Vietnam. c.1820)

THE VIETNAM BOX
Identity Lost, Truth Revealed

A case of mistaken identity can be flattering or discouraging, sometimes annoying, and occasionally deadly. My relatives and I are often mistaken for being 'Chinese,' thus dismissing our thousand-year-old culture and heritage. For many, the thought of Vietnam conjures unsettling images of war and brutality.

But I was crafted far from such notions, in the 'Mother of Pearl Inlay Village' of Chuon Ngo, located in Phu Xuyen district, about 40 km from Vietnam's capital, Hanoi. Chuon Ngo village has been renowned for its mastery of mother-of-pearl (MOP) inlaying for thousands of years.

The craft of MOP in Vietnam traces back to 1009 AD, founded by Truong Cong Thanh, a distinguished military leader and scholar during the 11th century. Alongside his contributions on the battlefield, Truong Cong Thanh became captivated by the craft, gathering innovations and ideas during his travels. Remarkably, MOP inlay has not only survived to this day but now sustains 95% of Chuon Ngo's 1,700 villagers, lifting many out of poverty. Master craftsmen from this village were once commissioned to produce trays and furniture for the royal court, and MOP inlaid furniture became a symbol of affluence. The intricate designs—some with pieces no larger than a fingernail—take years to perfect.

Raw materials for the craft, including shells of snails and pearls, come from various regions in Vietnam and are also imported from places like Hong Kong, Singapore, and Indonesia.

The process of creating MOP inlay is complex, different from any wood inlay techniques seen in the West. The iridescent materials are harvested from snails and mollusks, with snail shell pieces reflecting different colors from each angle, while pearl shells present a uniform color like pure white. Together, they create a magical contrast—white storks standing against the brilliant fluttering of kingfishers and butterflies.

After soaking and flattening the shells, artisans carefully cut out shapes using fine hand saws. The smaller details, such as plant tendrils and insect legs, are as thin as a human hair, requiring extraordinary precision. Many pieces break during this delicate process, but the artisans waste no time lamenting—another piece is cut to replace the lost one. After these tiny pieces are carved, they are fitted into recesses routed out of the wood, then glued into place, a tricky endeavor, especially when dealing with oily woods like rosewood, which resist adhesives due to heat and humidity.

The artistry does not stop with inlaying. In Vietnam, MOP is often engraved and filled with black ink, giving the designs depth and life. This extra step of engraving is rarely seen in modern tourist-trade pieces but remains a signature of masterwork. After the engraving, the wood is polished to seal the design, much like the fine inlaid metalwork seen in French furniture of the 17th century, such as that created by Charles-Andre Boulle.

Unlike Chinese and Japanese lacquerwork, which covers wood entirely, Vietnam's tradition allows the beauty of both wood and shell to be admired. Examples like me can be found at the National Museum of Vietnamese History in Hanoi.

I was a royal commission—my rarity owes much to my unusual octagonal shape and my ivory knob. Crafted just before the dawn of the Nguyen dynasty, I date back to the late 18th century when hinges and metal locks were not widely available to village artisans. For this reason, I have no hinges on my lid, and my lock is a mere decorative escutcheon, a nod to Western designs that were becoming popular among those desiring a secure box.

Compared to others, the MOP adorning my surface is relatively sparse, allowing the viewer to appreciate the rich beauty of the rosewood beneath. This backdrop for my decoration is one of the world's most exotic and expensive woods: Dalbergia odorifera, commonly known as fragrant rosewood or sweet-scented rosewood. Native to Southeast Asia, particularly China, Vietnam, and Laos, this wood is renowned for its sweet, floral scent, long-lasting fragrance, and stunning grain.

The fragrant rosewood I was made from has been cherished for centuries. Chinese emperors commissioned their imperial Ming palaces to be furnished with this precious wood. On Hainan Island, a particular strain known as Huanghuali (yellow flowering pear) became particularly prized, fetching high prices at auctions in the West. The wood was used for exquisite furniture, cabinetry, and fine musical instruments.

However, fragrant rosewood has been overexploited and is now listed as an endangered species. International conservation agreements like CITES (Convention on International Trade in Endangered Species of Wild Fauna and Flora) now protect it from illegal logging and trade. In Vietnam, the fragrant *rosewood tree was historically sought for its beauty and aromatic properties, used to build temples, palaces, and ancestral homes. Today, efforts to conserve Dalbergia odorifera have led to logging bans and conservation programs that promote sustainable management.*

Though a few Dalbergia odorifera trees remain in Vietnam, their numbers have dramatically dwindled. The species is now endangered, and restoring its habitat, along with enforcing strict protection measures, is vital to ensuring its long-term survival.

The tree that was felled to create me did so in 1780—before the rise of the Nguyen dynasty— during the Le Dynasty, which ruled Vietnam from 1428 to 1788. The Le Dynasty was a golden age of governance, literature, art, and Buddhism. I was proud to have been crafted in such a flourishing era and to have found myself in the possession of a family closely tied to royalty.

The Nguyen Dynasty, however, would eventually come under French control. Following the Sino-French War (1884-1885), the French established full colonial control over Vietnam, imposing changes that shaped Vietnam's cities, including Hanoi, where I remained. Though the French conquest is often seen as a period of turmoil, it also gave rise to an intellectual and artistic renaissance in Hanoi.

Julien Duvall, a French antiquarian, found me in one of Hanoi's bustling markets. By then, I had witnessed the tumult of history. Julien wasn't just an antiquarian—he dabbled in espionage, gathering intelligence for the French military. But his poor attempts to play spy led to tragedy. Mistaken for a professional spy by a Chinese underground group, Julien was assassinated in cold blood. At the moment of his death, he had just opened my lid to offer a client a whiff of the fragrance still locked inside. A bullet rang out, ending his life and leaving me with only a small scar.

Julien's belongings, including me, were sent to his sister in Vannes, France. She never fully understood his need for adventure or far-flung places, but she cherished the occasional letters he sent, which now sat next to me in her parlor.

There is never true closure when a life is reduced to a few mementos. They speak of a past, but only in whispers, while we—the objects that journey through time—carry on, witnesses to the lives and events that once were.

To confuse a Vietnamese box with a Chinese one or mistake one type of rosewood for another may seem like a small error, often born of ignorance, but sometimes, as in Julien's case, mistaken identity can have fatal consequences.

THE PALMWOOD BOX

From Riches to Ruin

THE PALMWOOD BOX (c. 1920)
From Riches to Ruin

Trinket box of dark streaked dense oil palm wood. Made by craftsmen using the wood of local palm oil palms. Yogyakarta, Central Java, Indonesia. c.1920.

THE PALMWOOD BOX
From Riches to Ruin

Come, children. Gather round, and I will tell you a story about growing up and how things don't always work out the way we planned.

Once upon a time, in a lush corner of West Africa, there stood a group of palm trees. Among them was a spirited coconut palm, known by the name of Coco (that's me, folks), and his faithful friend, a palm oil palm whose botanical title was *Elaeis guineensis*, but I affectionately called him cousin Eli. Their tale began in the very heart of a land where Eli's ancestors had been cultivated for countless generations. And though my own family hailed from distant corners of the world, I found myself here, swept up in an exotic adventure alongside Eli.

Under the sun's warm embrace and blankets of starlit nights, we flourished. Birds of all feathers and hues were attracted to us. Palm swifts, skilled builders, crafted delicate nests beneath our fronds, weaving their homes with the finesse of aerial architects. The rose-ringed parakeets, their vibrant plumage shimmering against the surroundings, feasted on fruits and left behind laughter that echoed through the rustling leaves. My heart swelled with joy each time the lively myna bird visited, its inquisitive eyes and constant chatter filling the air.

But among this lively avian congregation, there was one who stood apart—dark, common, enigmatic, and wise in his mischievous way. Drongo was famous for his skill in mimicry and incessant chatter. With eerie precision, he'd mimic the call of an eagle to startle nearby foraging meerkats. As the panicked creatures fled to their burrows, Drongo would swoop down and snatch their food, his devious plan executed to perfection. Drongo, wise and shrewd, didn't limit his antics to food alone. More relevant to our story, he shared his unconventional philosophy with cousin Eli, painting a world where survival meant taking from others, regardless of the means.

Once, Drongo whispered to cousin Eli that his destiny was to be felled and transformed into a box. Fear and anxiety gnawed at Eli's heart, prompting him to consider fleeing his impending fate. It was rumored that the British were planning a journey for Eli and his kin to the Far East, where they would be encouraged to produce palm oil to enhance the profits of an ever-greedy company.

The promise of profit and the callous beliefs of Drongo pushed Eli to question his destiny. He had no desire to be converted into a box. I watched my friend's inner turmoil, unable to quell the storm brewing within Eli's leaves. And so, against the backdrop of rustling palm fronds and the luxury of tropical life, the destinies of these two palm trees unfolded—a tale of friendship, choices, and the whispered secrets of the enigmatic Drongo.

The main motivation for bringing the palm oil palm to Asia was to establish plantations and expand the production of palm oil, which was in high demand as a cooking oil, soap ingredient, and lubricant for machinery. The Industrial Revolution in Europe was hungry for all of these. The tropical climate and fertile soils of Southeast Asia proved to be ideal for palm oil cultivation, leading to the successful establishment of large-scale palm oil plantations in the region.

During the British colonial era, British planters brought the palm oil palm from West Africa to their colonies in Southeast Asia, especially Malaysia and Indonesia, and also to India. They were primarily interested in its potential as a cash crop due to the increasing demand for palm oil in the industrializing world. The Dutch played a crucial role in transporting the palm oil palm to Southeast Asia by bringing the plant to their colonies, particularly in Indonesia, where the climate and soil conditions were favorable for palm oil production. Finally, the French introduced the palm oil palm to Indochina (present-day Vietnam, Cambodia, and Laos).

Eli decided to be included in the British consignment to India and convinced me to join him. This was easily done because one palm looks much like another, especially in their juvenile stage. Eli suspected that many old-growth trees and tropical forests would be cut down to make room for him and his friends, but it didn't matter to him because he was persuaded by Drongo's argument that self-fulfillment rules.

And so it was that cousin Eli and I were transplanted, along with many of his siblings, to a new area that had been cleared to make space for them. Although I was included in the shipment, I was separated on arrival to join other coconut palms. Separation is something experienced by all migrants. It can become a state of mind, dominating emotions and leading to feelings of emptiness, nostalgia, or a desire for reconnection. Although we were separated, we managed to stay in touch, though memories of Africa were soon replaced by our experiences in India. Even so, in old age, I would think wistfully of my early days as a small plant, lovingly cultivated side-by-side with Eli, and the incessant chatter of Drongo.

At that time, no one was concerned about deforestation, habitat destruction, or its impact on biodiversity and local communities. Those matters would only become topics of concern many decades into the future, but I clearly recall how Eli developed a strong feeling of guilt and shame that his growth and survival came at the cost of many, many ancient tropical hardwood trees. For untold generations, they had hosted colonies of birds, monkeys, and insects, all of whom died to make room for the fleshy, oil-producing fruit of the palm oil palm.

So it was that Eli and I went to India, he believing that if his presence produced a beneficial product from his fruit, then the eviction of the old residents was justified.

But after a few short years, Eli's fruit-producing days came to an end, and he overheard the farm manager saying that he and his friends would be cleared to make room for new, younger stock. Although this upset him, there was nothing he could do about it, and inevitably, he was cut down.

Often overlooked is the poignant truth that a tree is, in its own right, a sentient being, its passing to be lamented and mourned as any other living entity. Its moment of departure remains as enigmatic as it is in the realm of humans. Just as the human heart ceases its rhythm, the lungs cease their pulse, and the brain's melody fades, so does the tree undergo a silent transition. Ideally, one envisions this as an instantaneous metamorphosis, each cessation harmoniously merging with the others, yet reality seldom aligns with ideals.

Eli, once vibrant in the embrace of the Indian sun, encountered the first cut of the axe with a sensation akin to a human's first grasp of pain. A fraction of his rising sap, like a sudden, stifled sigh, met an abrupt disruption. Subsequent strikes echoed with a brutal chorus, severing the flow of life-giving nourishment to his roots, which anchored him and communicated with his neighbors.

With every axe's bite, Eli's heartwood—his very core—fought to sustain his towering form. A valiant struggle played out in those moments, like a warrior striving to bear the weight of his helmet and shield as the battle continued. Then, as the agony peaked, an anguished lament of splintering fibers and rending sinews echoed through the air, a macabre symphony of breaking dreams and extinguished life.

However, the finale wasn't swift. The forces of fate expressed the narrative with measured cruelty. Like a captive tormented in stages, Eli endured. Just as the tormentor steps back to relish the pain he has provoked, Eli's agony lingered. Enzymes were summoned, twisting his fronds into contorted shapes—a desperate gambit to stem the tide of transpiration, as if clutching onto fleeting life. Alas, even this poignant tactic failed to alter his inexorable plight, his impending fate as an arboreal spirit.

The fellers, armed with a repertoire of tools and the conviction of their purpose, returned with grim resolve. Axes, honed to gleaming edges, cleaved his trunk into manageable fragments, each section a chapter in the melancholic tale of his passing. Carried away by hands as indifferent as the wind, they left behind an emptiness—a void that once was home to his mighty presence.

His crown, once a refuge for Drongo and a sanctuary of shade for many, was now destined for an elemental pyre. Drawn towards the fire's inferno, it succumbed to metamorphosis, becoming ephemeral plumes of smoke and soot. Driven by the wind's capricious whim, his remnants dispersed—a fleeting reunion with the boundless sky.

Only when his roots, those tendrils that once anchored his being, were wrenched from the soil could the world acknowledge his final farewell. A quiet conclusion—a chapter's end—no triumphant crescendo, no dramatic flourish. Just a series of moments, each carrying its own weight, each inching towards an inevitable conclusion.

In the hush of that eternal departure, the tree's final breath merged with the symphony of the ages— a poignant reminder of the shared fragility and fleeting nature of existence.

In a nearby village lived a woodworker. Generally, he made furniture, but occasionally, he made small boxes. He usually worked in timber and was often asked to craft small items from sandalwood, but he was very attracted to the crazy patterns within the wood of palm trees.

Technically, palms aren't trees at all, belonging as they do to the grass family. It follows that their 'wood' isn't really wood because it has no annual rings and doesn't come from a tree. But its alternating dark and light stripes make for dramatic patterns and material that is hard and strong. The woodworker decided he would use some of Eli's wood to make a box, lining the lid with sandalwood from the nearby copse. The fragrance of sandalwood is enduring and would provide a pleasant experience for the owner every time the box was opened.

It is a wonderful mystery how trees can persist in spirit more effectively than humans. As part of Eli's trunk was fashioned into the box by the craftsman, I became aware of his spirit. But this was not a happy reunion. Eli was undergoing a process of reincarnation, but he was inconsolable over the sacrifices others had made for his brief life. He seemed to think that his current suffering was an atonement for previous wrongs.

I tried to explain that the oil from his fruit had found its way into many useful products, such as lubricants for the rapidly growing machinery and industrial sectors of the 19th century. It provided an essential lubricating agent for the steam engines and machines powering the Industrial Revolution. The increased demand for palm oil as an industrial lubricant contributed to its economic importance. The British soap and candle industry, which experienced substantial growth during the 19th century, relied on palm oil as a key ingredient.

Palm oil was also useful in the textile industry for the processing of cotton and other fibers. It was used as a sizing agent, improving the texture and strength of fabrics. As the textile industry expanded during the Industrial Revolution, demand for palm oil grew as well. It also found application in cooking and as an ingredient in various food products. Later, it was incorporated into cosmetics, soaps, and personal care products due to its emollient properties.

Despite my attempts to paint a positive picture of palm oil and its benefits, Eli could only focus on the destruction he had caused in pursuit of global trade and the colonial expansion of the British Empire. I listened carefully to Eli's anguish, and it seemed that sharing memories of the old-growth forest we once called home nourished us both. It is generally helpful for the elderly to deal with the present by revisiting memories and ghosts of times past. Through this process, we were able to formulate our hopes for the future. We decided to embrace our destinies and focus on spreading awareness about responsible and sustainable palm cultivation. If the world becomes concerned about the damage caused by reckless palm oil production, something good may finally be achieved.

Many years passed, and I forged an unexpected spiritual friendship with the same clever Drongo. Curiosity finally got the better of me, and one day, I posed the question that had long lingered in my mind.

"Drongo," I began, "why did you frighten cousin Eli with tales of becoming a box? Why play such tricks?"

Drongo, perched high on a swaying frond, fixed his intelligent eyes on me. "Ah, young Coco," he croaked, "you speak of ideals, but ideals don't feed an empty belly."

I responded with unwavering resolve, "Yet ideals shape who we become. Our choices echo through time, shaping the legacy we leave behind."

Drongo, perched thoughtfully with his ebony feathers catching the sunlight, continued, "Ah," he crooned, "I believed a hint of his fate might spark an awareness of life's transient nature. Though I didn't reveal his journey to India, I meant to remind him that paths can be both unexpected and transformative."

"But," I countered, "if he'd known, he might not have embarked on that journey at all."

Drongo nodded sagely. "True," he admitted, "but we cannot entirely elude our fate. Eli's tale didn't conclude with a box. That box, now a century and a half old, holds him still—a testament to the delicate balance between progress and the preservation of nature's beauty."

He continued, "Eli's transformation into palm wood echoes not only the legacy of the palm oil palm but also that of the date palm, another esteemed member of your family. Above all, that sandalwood-lined box weaves all your journeys together—coconut, palm oil, and date—all united by shared experiences and aspirations for a better world."

As the two palms became migrants journeying to distant lands, they realized their destiny was to impart essential lessons. The paths they had chosen intersected with human pursuits, whispering caution about environmental destruction and the fragility of nature's ecosystems.

"Fate may be known," Drongo mused, "but destiny? Destiny is a dance with life, where individuals shape their futures and influence their surroundings. It is a purposeful stride forward."

In essence, fate extends a guiding hand from afar, while destiny empowers individuals to wield their own compass, guiding their life's narrative. The coconut palm and the palm oil palm parted ways, grounded in the certainty that their connection would endure through shared tales of growth and the collective dream of a greener tomorrow.

In the end, Eli's story taught that seizing control over one's immediate fate can lead to short-term success, even profit. Yet, the grander destiny lay in participating in the education of humankind—nurturing awareness of environmental havoc. Eli's journey, forever intertwined with mine, underscored the power of destiny—an active, purposeful journey fueled by choices and the urge to make the world a better place.

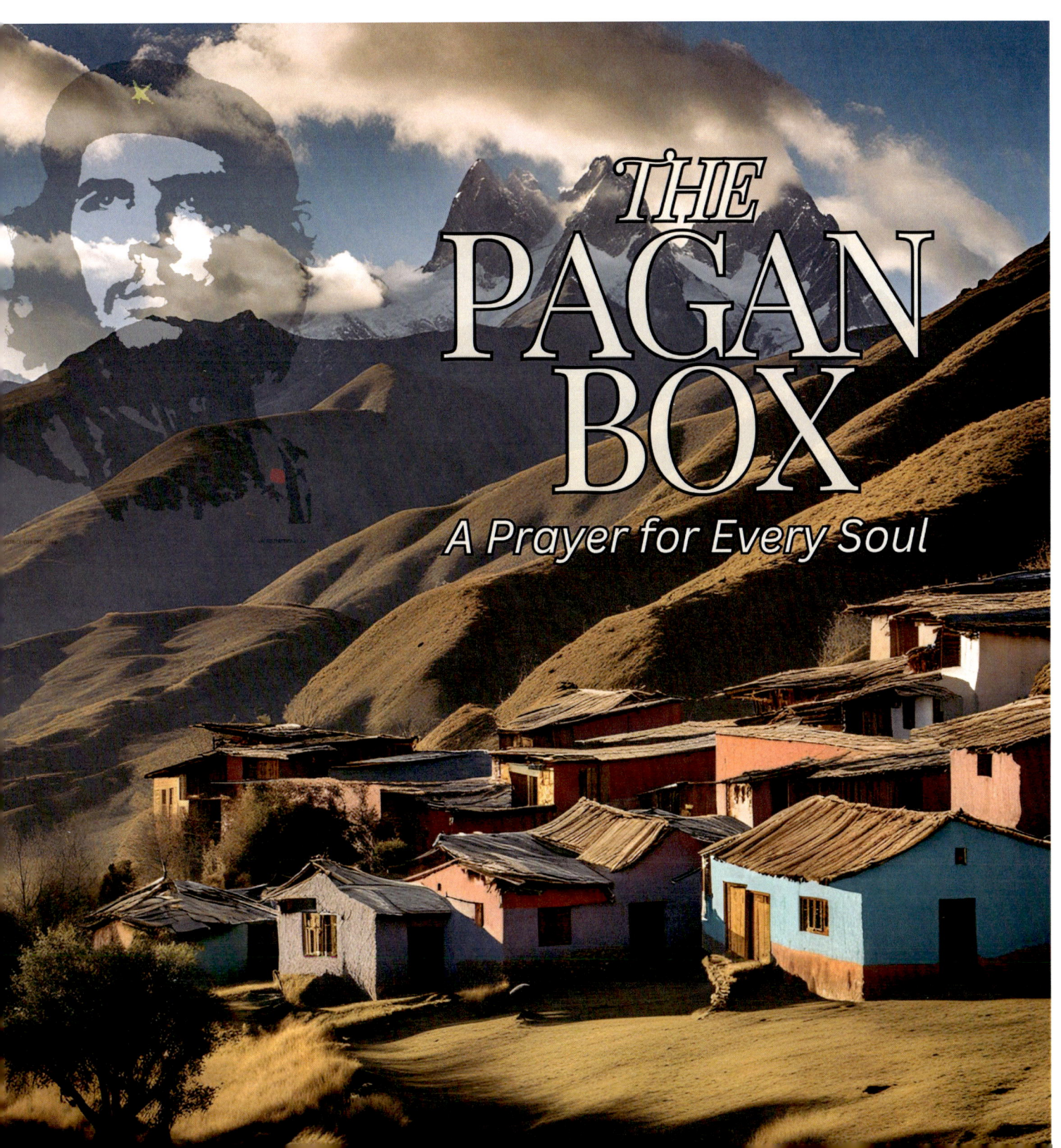

THE PAGAN BOX
A Prayer for Every Soul

A PAGAN BOX (c. 1970)
A Prayer for Every Soul

Hollow devotional statue made of Bolivian mahogany from Yungas region. Made by Aymara craftsman beside Lake Titicaca depicting the monumental stone monolith at Tiwanaku. Copacabana, Bolivia. c.1970.

A PAGAN BOX
A Prayer for Every Soul

It is 1968, and the place is Bolivia, where Che Guevara's socialism had clashed with Bolivian nationalism, leading to his death the previous October.
The U.S. Peace Corps, established by John F. Kennedy, was active on several projects in the country, while the author also served there as a volunteer with the United Nations.

Towering among the ruins of a temple on the high Altiplano of Bolivia stands a twenty-foot-tall stone monolith, a mysterious statue and silent witness to an ancient civilization, now abandoned like the lake whose shores it once bordered. Tiwanaku, also spelled Tiahuanaco, is an archaeological site almost 10 miles from Lake Titicaca, the largest and highest freshwater lake in the world. In that arid place, the air is thin. At 12,000 feet, it's not a place for anyone in a hurry.

But Harry was in a hurry. As a Peace Corps volunteer, he had been sent on a two-year assignment to Bolivia along with three friends. Their project was to help improve education and literacy in rural schools of the Altiplano, that vast and featureless plain between the capital, La Paz, and the snow-capped Cordillera of the high Andes. This involved teaching Aymara Indian children who spoke little Spanish and no English. He was also tasked with educating teachers in modern skills that he had brought from Connecticut.

We met in Oruro, that godforsaken mining town where the air is so thin it fails to bring the warmth of the sun into the shadows. Until 16 years previously, the town and community had been owned by the Patiño family, who exercised a monopoly over the tin that was mined there. As a British volunteer with the United Nations, my official project was to teach chemistry at the University of La Paz. For relaxation, I also played violin with the Bolivian National Symphony Orchestra on an amateur basis. During that time, we had the pleasant task of visiting Oruro to perform a concert in celebration of the 16th anniversary of the nationalization of the tin mines.

The orchestra arrived one evening in a couple of buses, which dropped us off a short distance from the hotel where we would be staying. We couldn't be taken directly to the hotel because the road was unmade and unsuitable for wheeled vehicles. But that walk was priceless. We were welcomed by rows of curious children and adults who had never seen an orchestra or even Western musical instruments before. They were only familiar with local instruments like the charango, a plucked instrument made from an armadillo shell strummed like a banjo, the guitar, and a drum-like bombo, together with the zampoña pipes. The bombo would be beaten to drive the rhythm while the breathy zampoña pan pipes intoned a wistfully jolly tune. As I was the only Westerner in the orchestra (apart from conductor Gerry Brown, also a Peace Corps volunteer), I attracted more attention than most. Everyone assumed that I was carrying a small guitar in my violin case, but the excitement had to wait until the concert the following day.

Harry, who was also harboring a secret, formed part of that welcoming crowd, although I was too busy soaking in the local color to notice him. The remoteness and simplicity of the place became apparent when we discovered that the only washing facility in the hotel was a cold tap in the patio. A shower was out of the question, but I wouldn't have had it any other way.

The concert was free, so the hall where it was held was packed. After a few initial words of welcome and formal pleasantries, it was decided that the leader of each orchestra section would play a few notes to introduce his musical instrument to the enthralled audience. It fell to me, as leader of the string section, to play a scale or two on my violin, augmented by a trill and a flourish, which made me feel like a latter-day Paganini. This simple articulation was greeted with rapturous applause by an audience who had never heard the like before.

Harry had accompanied a group of teenage pupils, traditionally dressed in ponchos and knitted headgear with earflaps. After the concert, they formed part of the excited committee that received us enthusiastically as we exited the makeshift theater. Meeting him afforded me a rare opportunity to speak English with someone. I asked if Harry and his friends ever made the trip to La Paz. Seemingly, they made the trip once every couple of months when there would be a Peace Corps reunion characterized by raucous drinking and singing. I learned this after I was invited to attend one of their sessions on Harry's next trip to the Andean capital.

I had occasion to be grateful to Harry after I made a trip out of La Paz to the headwaters of the Amazon—one of those trips encouraged to help us become more familiar with our host country. The wonderful thing about La Paz is that, although it is situated at 12,000 feet on a barren plain surrounded by mountains, you can travel an hour and a half over flat, arid land without seeing a single tree. Eventually, the road led to Copacabana (the beach in Brazil appropriated the name!), situated on the shores of Lake Titicaca. It was, and still is, home to the shrine of the famous Virgin of Copacabana, the patron saint of Bolivia.

A bus or truck journey in the opposite direction led to the subtropical region of the Yungas, by way of the infamous Death Road (El Camino de La Muerte), where banana and coffee plantations could be found. But my journey had taken me much further, to the headwaters of the Amazon River. For a city dweller, every step of this adventure through the dark recesses of the jungle presented an intense feeling of mystery and wonder. Here, the heavy air embraced me with a warm, moist caress. Gazing upwards, the towering trees formed a natural cathedral, their colossal trunks reaching skyward like ancient pillars or monumental statues, carrying an aura of timelessness.

This world of monkeys, macaws, and shamans left an impression that this ecosystem was not just a spectacle but a fragile web of life, intricately connected and interdependent; Bolivia's yin to the Altiplano's yang.

Upon my return to La Paz, I was utterly and inexplicably exhausted. I couldn't walk half a block without needing to sit, rest, and catch my breath. The Bolivian University doctor was no help, attributing my listlessness to the altitude and recommending aspirin and a couple of days in bed. This had no beneficial effect on my condition.

When I mentioned this to Harry a few days later on his next visit to the capital, he took me in hand and insisted we go immediately to the Peace Corps doctor, who would sort me out. The doctor took blood samples for analysis, and shortly afterward, called me with the results. I had contracted typhus, typhoid, and paratyphoid, all of which could have killed me if I had not received the appropriate injections before leaving for my assignment. With this diagnosis, the cure was quick, and I survived to tell the tale.

The same could not be said of the monolith of Tiwanaku. Although it survived, it was a silent witness, unable to recount its story or that of the people who had created it. It was the opposite of us volunteers, who were expected to tell our stories daily.

There is a story the Bolivians tell about themselves. When God created the Earth, He told the angels that He would place vast amounts of gold in the riverbeds of Tipuani, vast amounts of silver in the mountains of Potosi—so much that the Spanish conquistadores would use it as a world currency and destabilize their own economy. Oil and natural gas would be found in the region of Santa Cruz. He said He would enrich the landscape with fertile ground capable of producing every crop from potatoes on the

Altiplano to the hardwood trees in the tropical rainforests. At this point, the angels said to God, 'But how can you indulge one country with so many natural riches? It doesn't seem fair.' And God replied, 'Oh, but you haven't seen the people I plan to put there.' Bolivians are quick to add, with a laugh, that they have a true democracy, and everyone has the right to be president, even if it's only for a day or two.

Harry and I completed our terms at roughly the same time, and as a parting gift, he presented me with a thoughtful but cumbersome and practically useless item—a box made of fine mahogany in the shape of that monolith, with a lid that lifted off. At two feet high, it was difficult to know what to do with it, but it was so iconic and typical of that wonderful country that I had to find a way to bring it home. To me, it wasn't silent. It whispered the story of its birth in Copacabana, where an artisan had crafted it from jungle mahogany. It had been gifted to Harry, under strict secrecy, by the craftsman who made it. Harry was duty-bound to accept it, but finding it too voluminous to keep with him, he, in turn, gifted it to me. I learned more details because wood speaks to Wood. Here is the story told by the statue.

In the summer of 1969, a woodcarver in Copacabana, the town on the shores of Lake Titicaca (after which its famous namesake in Brazil was named), had a dream. His name was Luis Yupanbi—Lucho to his friends. In the dream, the Virgin of Copacabana, the patron saint of Bolivia, told him to make a statuette of the Tiwanaku monolith, a symbol of pre-Christian idolatry. Lucho was chosen for this task because it was his ancestor who had carved the original image of the Virgin of Copacabana in 1582. The idea was that the image of the 'pagan' monolith should be burned by the villagers as a way to atone for loose ways incompatible with the teachings of the Catholic Church. Such an act of desecration was meant to redirect their faith back to the 'true' church. The war in the idolatry stakes was about to engage in another skirmish.

Until then, if anyone fell into the lake, no one would rescue them because it was considered an offering to the lake. In another act of opportunistic sacrifice, once a year, young men would trek up to a nearby glacier and engage in a ritual fight. Not all who went up returned. Those who didn't were revered for their sacrifice. These practices could be traced back to the Incas, who held this terrain in special regard, and whose beliefs the Spanish colonialists had worked so hard to stamp out.

Lucho devoted himself to crafting a replica of the old idol, pouring countless hours into meticulously working the finest mahogany—*Swietenia macrophylla*—sourced from the forested lowlands where his ancestors had once lived before being evicted long ago. He carefully replicated the intricate details and symbols found on the original monolith. He poured his heart and soul into the project, ensuring that every line and curve mirrored the grandeur of the ancient sculpture. But when the time came for the ritualistic immolation, Lucho couldn't bear to see his handiwork destroyed. Moreover, he was certain that the old spirits who revered the original monolith would take revenge on the act of impiety that he had provoked. Underpaid local archaeologists had sold the golden treasures they discovered to foreign diplomats, who spirited them out of the country in diplomatic pouches. Better not to antagonize the old spirits further. So, how to resolve the dilemma?

He found a solution involving two members of the Peace Corps stationed in Oruro. They had ventured to the historic town of Copacabana to pay homage to the patron saint of Bolivia, a small statue of the Virgin housed in a 17th-century Spanish colonial basilica. They marveled at her bejeweled attire. Each day, she was adorned in fresh clothes and accessories, with enough variety to ensure her garments wouldn't repeat for 365 days.

Their hearts stirred with an unconventional notion. They contemplated the region's poverty, and the idea dawned upon them that perhaps those opulent gifts, tokens of adoration from the wealthy, could serve a greater purpose if liquidated. The proceeds could be distributed among the needy. Yet, as they gazed upon the adoring congregation, hands clasped in prayer, rosary beads slipping through weathered fingers, doubts crept in.

These humble people owned little in material wealth, but they possessed something profound— faith. They had an exalted entity to whom they could pour out their hopes and fears, a motherly figure who had suffered as they had. She was a conduit, their solace, the keeper of their innermost prayers, and linked to her son in ways they couldn't fathom. Stripping her of these gifts would be akin to robbing them of their most cherished connection.

As the volunteers observed and reflected, they didn't realize that Lucho had them in his sights. With a heart conflicted between duty and faith, he decided to put his plan into action. He approached the Peace Corps visitors and asked one of them, Harry, if he would accept the statue as a gift and carry it away with him to Oruro. He asked only one favor in return—that he not share with anyone how or where he had acquired the statue. Harry graciously accepted both the statue and the condition. He took it with him to Oruro, where it remained until Harry was ready to return to the United States.

At that moment, Harry gifted me the statue, omitting any mention of its true origins. I accepted it in good faith, though with some apprehension due to its bulk, which added to my already heavy luggage. It wasn't until I began packing that I discovered the cap was detachable, revealing a hollow interior where I could store other items. As a practical box, its storage capacity was minimal, but its value became immeasurable once I learned its story. And so, the statue embarked on its clandestine journey, far from its homeland. The revered idol left Copacabana and Bolivia, not in smoke, but tucked away in a suitcase.

And so, half a century later and several thousand miles away, that proud wooden statue continues its silent vigil—a secret guardian of the hopes of a vanished people. It serves as a living reminder that faith, in all its forms, transcends time and place. Whether Christian or pagan, it speaks to the same deep-seated need for connection to something greater than ourselves. The wooden copy of a stone impression of a disembodied deity—fragile in its reality, yet unyielding in its significance. It whispers that faith, no matter how distant from its origin, remains a treasure beyond measure, a living entity that must be nurtured daily lest it fade into the void it seeks to fill.

THE SEDAN BOX

Divided by Tyranny

THE SEDAN BOX (c. 1620)
Divided by Tyranny

A sedan box of northern elm wood, lacquered inside and out then inlaid with engraved bone. Made by Ming dynasty craftsmen of unusual form designed to carry important documents and fit between the carry poles of a sedan chair. Beijing, China. c1620.

THE SEDAN BOX
Divided by Tyranny

A 400-year-old Chinese jiaoxiang box, once belonging to a Ming dynasty scholar, bears witness to the rise and fall of powerful figures throughout history who have divided their nations through civil war. From the Ming dynasty's bureaucratic refinements to the brutal reigns of 20th-century dictators, the box serves as a silent reminder of the cyclical nature of tyranny. Its intricate designs, once a symbol of elite culture, now warn us of the dangers of complacency. The story underscores that, despite historical lessons, the threat of authoritarianism persists, demanding constant vigilance to prevent its resurgence.

In the affairs of nations, it sometimes becomes an unavoidable necessity for a leader to steer his country into war, be it in defense against external aggression or in the pursuit of expansion. Yet, there exists a special circle of hell reserved for those who, in their insatiable thirst for personal glorification and enrichment, choose to sow discord within their own land, pitting brother against brother and son against father. This tale concerns two unelected leaders whose names are etched in the annals of recent history but whose legacies now risk fading into oblivion. One was a tyrant responsible for the deaths of millions, and the other, a lesser monster by comparison, yet no less sinister, whose rule cost the lives of hundreds of thousands.

The nations that bore the brunt of such civil strife were China and Spain. Authoritarian leaders, with cruel disregard for human life, unleashed torrents of death through starvation, forced labor, concentration camps, mass executions, and torture. These horrors were perpetrated in full view of a world that, paralyzed by the sanctity of national sovereignty, stood idly by, deeming these atrocities mere domestic matters.

This is the story of one of them.

Mr. Lu had already been dead for three days when his neighbors finally discovered him. The modest room where he lay was shrouded in silence, his lifeless body stretched upon a simple bed. In his arms, he cradled a box—his pride and joy. It was not just any box; it was a jiaoxiang, a document case of ancient origin lovingly restored by Mr. Lu's own hands and now the centerpiece of his life. Neighbors knew of his skill in breathing new life into old boxes. He often showed them the fruits of his work, and they marveled. But he would always say: "Ah, but one day I will show you a box like no other." Upon seeing the box he caressed in death, there was little doubt that this was the one he had referred to so often.

The box, with its peculiar design to fit between the carry poles of a sedan chair, had seen two centuries pass since its creation during the Ming dynasty, circa 1590. Crafted in the imperial workshop, it bore the marks of the finest artisans—carpenters, ivory workers, and lacquer specialists—who collaborated to create scenes of Ming officials reveling in the luxury afforded by their station. They were easily recognizable by their hanfu, the traditional dress imposed by the Han rulers of the Ming dynasty. The exterior was cloaked in black lacquer, with ivory figures and landscapes adorning its surface. The interior was lined with red cinnabar lacquer, a symbol of long life and a marker of scholarly refinement.

To the Chinese scholar, the red lacquer within was more than mere decoration; it was a symbol of intellectual and moral virtue, resonating with the Confucian ideals held in the highest esteem. The box was originally intended for a scholar-official close to the imperial court, used to transport documents of great importance, perhaps even bearing the seal of the emperor himself. Its original owner, Mr. Zhang, served as the personal secretary to Emperor Wanli during a time of great prosperity for the empire, though the wealth of the few was built on the backs of the impoverished many.

This story, like the box itself, is a relic of the past, yet its message is timeless. The Ming scholars and officials depicted in ivory lived lives of luxury and power, while the vast majority of the population toiled in poverty to sustain the feudal system. The parallels to modern times are clear, for in every era there are those who rise to power through the suffering of others, and history has shown that memories are short. The dangers of imperialistic dictatorships are ever-present, and the lessons of the past must not be forgotten, lest we allow such horrors to repeat.

In the late summer of 1966, the so-called 'Cultural Revolution' was gathering momentum in China. It was a quiet evening in our house just before the Red Guards came to loot it. The windows of the study where I was kept were open, and the fragrance of the flowers in the garden wafted in. We heard the engine of a truck in the distance grow louder and waited to hear it drive past, but it didn't. It stopped outside the house, and very quickly afterward, there was a loud banging at the door. Many fists were pounding, accompanied by hysterical voices shouting and ordering that the door be opened.

"Open the door! Can't you hear us?"

It was intimidating, and my master, who was alone in the house, quietly tried to maintain a calm demeanor as he went to the door to confront the people. There were between 30 to 40 senior high school students led by two men and one much older woman. They seemed to be the teachers who generally accompanied the Red Guards when they looted private homes. They crowded into the hall, knocking over plant pots and vases of flowers, which they trampled underfoot. The leading Red Guard, a gangly youth with angry eyes, stepped forward and shouted, "We are the Red Guards. We have come to take revolutionary action against you!"

These intruders could all have been family members and, in better times, would have been warmly received. But now, they appeared as savages with anger replacing respect and civility.

My master held up a copy of the constitution, pointing out that it was forbidden to enter a private house without a search warrant. The young man snatched the document out of his hand and threw it on the floor. With his eyes blazing, he said, "The constitution is abolished. It was a document written by the revisionists within the Communist Party. We recognize only the teaching of the Great Leader Chairman Mao."

He then tore down a painting and replaced it with a sign on which was written a quotation from Mao Zedong: 'When the enemies with guns are annihilated, the enemies without guns still remain.' All of the Red Guards, like a nest of cockroaches, had scattered throughout the house, which had been beautifully cleaned and organized with everything in its correct place. Within minutes, items had been smashed, and the whole house desecrated. We now knew what rape felt like.

Many items like me, old and precious, were scooped up and taken to a room where we were set aside for some later fate. The master was told he must not enter that room again until the items contained within it had been confiscated by the Army working to satisfy the God, Mao Zedong. Their own free will had been eliminated and reprogrammed with the propaganda they had absorbed.

I overheard a brief conversation between one of the students and the older woman: "Ah, Li Wei, you seem troubled. What's on your mind?" asked the teacher.
"Teacher, I've been thinking... I don't want to become a Red Guard. The thought of raiding the homes of the elderly, destroying their treasures... it feels wrong. These people have done nothing to me, and yet,

we're supposed to take everything from them?"

"Li Wei, I understand your hesitation. But you must think of the greater good. The Great Helmsman has made it clear that for China to progress, we must rid ourselves of the old ways, the old ideas. These relics you speak of—they are symbols of a past that has no place in our new society."

"But what about the people? They're just... people. Shouldn't we respect their age, their wisdom?"

"Respect? That is exactly the problem. The old ways demand respect for things that hold us back, that keep us chained to a feudal past. The Great Helmsman requires us to be bold, to take action in the name of revolution. And besides, all your friends are joining the cause. Do you really want to be the one who stands apart, clinging to outdated values?"

"But... if I refuse, what will happen?"

"Refusal is not an option, Li Wei. You know that. To refuse is to be seen as a reactionary, someone who opposes progress. Is that how you want to be remembered? Alone, while your friends and comrades march forward in unity?"

Sighs "No, Teacher. I don't want to be left behind. I... I'll do it."

"Good. Remember, Li Wei, this is not just about you. It's about the future of our nation. You are part of something much larger, something that will be remembered for generations. Now go and do what must be done."

"Yes, Teacher. I understand now." *bows head* "For the revolution."

Peer pressure, authoritarian persistence, and the fear of ostracism had done their work.

Throughout the house, we could hear the sound of glass and crockery being shattered and heavy knocking on the walls. The noise intensified. It sounded almost as if the Red Guards were tearing the house down rather than merely looting its contents. What they were doing was collecting old things, which represented the old China, expecting to replace them with a new culture of socialism. That said, I'm sure it was apparent to them that we old things added value from which they could profit at some point.

I was sure I would be smashed to splinters. Such was the savagery of the invasion of a home belonging to a gentle, middle-class family. By good fortune, the next day I was driven off, along with many other items of antique furniture, to a musty old warehouse. At the time, I didn't know it, but I would remain here for several years, experiencing extremes of summer heat and the freezing cold of Shanghai winters. It was lucky that my previous restoration, 200 years earlier, had strengthened my corners, so my shape was retained, though parts of my lacquer finish cracked and detached.

Sometime during the 1970s, an intermediary named Chen Hai bribed the poorly paid guards and gained access to the warehouse with the intention of 'borrowing' a few items for study purposes. He was working for the American dealer Nathaniel Grayson, who was finding a ready market for Chinese antiques back home. The difficulty was exporting them, as we old things were designated as cultural treasures and rarely given export licenses. Once in his hands, Grayson had me painted dark brown and managed to spirit me away to San Francisco—far from the turmoil still ravaging China.

Tragically, Chen Hai was branded a 'rightist' by a neighbor during one of the neighborhood denunciation meetings, a common feature of the Cultural Revolution. A humiliating sign was hung around his neck, and he was forced to kneel and publicly apologize to those he had once considered friends. It was true that he had occasional dealings with foreigners, earning modest compensation, but Chen was a gentle and refined man undeserving of the torment he faced. His neighbors bore him no real ill will, but in the fevered atmosphere of the time, they felt compelled to demonstrate their loyalty to the Revolution Committee and Chairman Mao.

The world had gone mad. As the pain of wood splinters in his knees joined the screams of invective in his ears, he thought of the poor craft workers who had brought the box to life in that distant Beijing workshop. I was not only a symbol of luxury for the elite but also testimony to the skills of those who labored under stressful conditions to make their lives possible. Chen Hai found himself unable to navigate the ruthless dog-eat-dog reality that had taken hold. After the meeting, consumed by despair, he returned home and took his own life.

Grayson's extensive inventory of antiques was so vast that he never found the time to properly clean me up and offer me for sale. In 2005, his remaining possessions were auctioned in New York, where I was mistakenly cataloged as a musical instrument case. Although my purpose was misunderstood, my age was not in doubt. Lacquer applied to wood, with an intermediate layer of thin cloth, takes several centuries to develop an alligator-like craquelure. I caught the eye of an astute historian and scholar, specializing in Chinese antiquities. Drawing on her deep knowledge of the Ming chronicles, she recognized my true purpose and wasted no time in having me meticulously cleaned and restored. The restoration process revealed the intricate details of my decoration, showing the hanfu attire of the scholars, officials, and servants depicted on my surface. This period, when Han rulers dictated the dress code of all society members—from headwear to footwear—marked a clear social hierarchy and function, devoid of the pigtails that would later become mandatory under the Manchu rulers of the Qing dynasty.

Margaret, as my new owner was named, first established my age by identifying the eight Precious Things decorating my two ends. Chinese culture has recognized a hundred precious objects over the years, ranging from flaming pearls to upside-down bats, but usually, only the "Eight Treasures" or "Babao" are shown at one time. The precise selection has varied throughout history, but she was able to identify rhinoceros horns, the artemisia leaf, a ruyi scepter, a double lozenge, and some coral.

During the Ming Dynasty (1368–1644), symbols such as rhino horns, coral, and ruyi scepters were more prominent in art and decorative objects. The Ming Dynasty focused on symbolism related to power, protection, longevity, and prosperity, all of which these items represent. Rhino horns were highly valued for their supposed medicinal properties and as symbols of status. Coral was seen as a symbol of longevity and prosperity, while the ruyi scepter symbolized power and good fortune. The double lozenge (fangsheng or shuangshou) often represented longevity, and the artemisia leaf was associated with health and protection from evil.

In the Qing Dynasty (1644–1912), while some of these symbols remained in use, the cultural and artistic influences of the Manchu rulers led to shifts in symbolism and the favored items. For instance, Tibetan Buddhist symbolism became more prominent, with items like the endless knot, conch shell, and vase gaining significance.

Therefore, a set containing these specific items would likely be more characteristic of the Ming Dynasty, reflecting the symbolism and cultural values of that period.

As the cleaning progressed, Margaret identified my original owner from the scenes depicted in the ornate designs. While the images portrayed an idyllic Ming lifestyle, Margaret knew that Mr. Zhang, who commissioned me when he was appointed to the imperial court, was a reformer of the late Ming period. He championed the belief that public opinion outweighed individual interests, advocating for a political and administrative system where decision-making was informed by the collective wisdom of officials through questionnaires and voting ballots. In an attempt to curb the excesses of the corrupt officials surrounding the emperor, Zhang played a crucial role in implementing these voting and ballot systems for officer selection. During this time, I was frequently used to transport crucial documents back and forth before the emperor would give his seal of approval. Alas, Zhang's efforts were short-lived.

Evil and greed may be restrained for a time, but they are never truly eradicated. They merely bide their time, waiting to resurface when the moment is ripe.

In the quiet of her study, Margaret reflected on the troubled times from which I, the jiaoxiang, had recently escaped—China, only 30 years earlier. Estimates ranging from 40 to 80 million victims had died due to starvation, persecution, prison labor, and mass executions. Mao's government has been described as totalitarian, but that term alone could not convey the depth of suffering experienced by a populace unable to rest for a generation, never knowing who would be the next to be denounced, humiliated, or die of disease due to malnutrition.

In one of history's coincidences, the 'Great Helmsman' died in September 1976, quickly followed by General Francisco Franco in November of the same year. He had fought his way to dictatorship through the Civil War in Spain, which lasted three terrible years from 1936 to 1939. About 500,000 people lost their lives in the White Terror. Of these, around 200,000 died as the result of systematic killings, mob violence, torture, or other brutalities.

Margaret was struck by the fact that both modern dictators, Mao and Franco, died in the same year after reigns of terror enacted by turning one part of their populations against the other.

Authoritarian regimes have risen repeatedly throughout history, from the feudal lords of China to the "emperors" of modern times, like Mao and Franco. The 'good old days' were great for the few but not so great for the many. The past is never as distant as we think, and the danger of repeating it is always present. The box, once a symbol of power and wealth, now serves as a cautionary tale about the dangers of yearning for a bygone era without understanding the harsh realities that accompanied it. It serves as a reminder of the recurring nature of authoritarian rule, the suffering it causes, and the importance of vigilance to prevent the rise of new dictators.

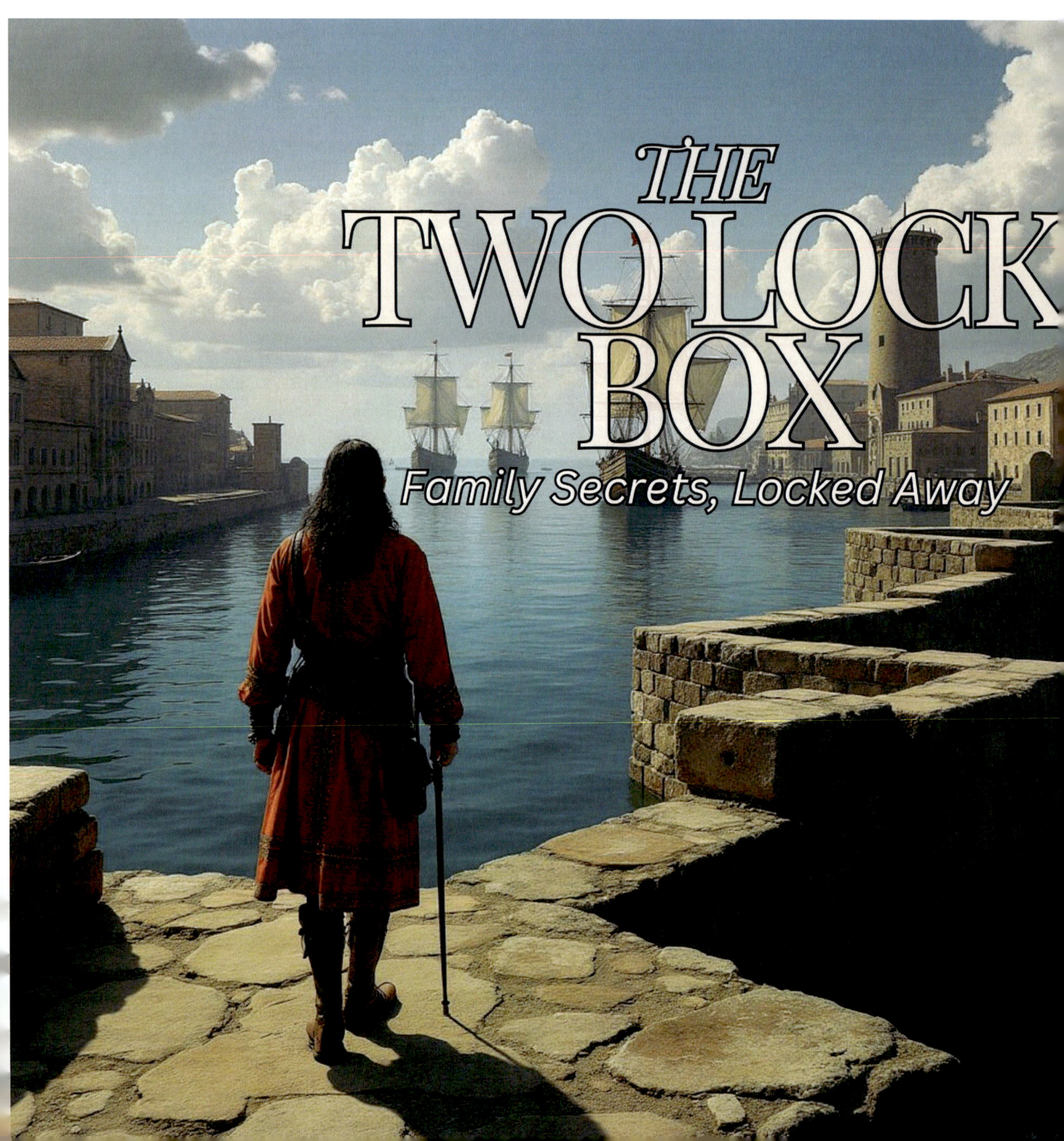

THE TWO LOCK BOX

Family Secrets, Locked Away

THE TWO LOCK BOX (c. 1650)
Family Secrets, Locked Away

Made of Andalusian Black pine from the Sierra Nevada, inlaid with walnut and provided with iron fittings. Made under contract by a cabinet maker who subcontracted the creation of a double lock requiring two different keys to operate it. Seville, Spain. c.1650.

THE TWO LOCK BOX
Family Secrets, Locked Away

How valuable or sensitive must something be to warrant two-step authentication?

Valuables are often secured in a box locked by a single key. But when two locks, each requiring a separate key, are necessary, it signals that what is being protected holds extraordinary value. Our antique two-lock box predates modern data protection methods like public and private key encryption and two-step verification—by 400 years!

In the 17th century, a dual-lock box requiring two separate keys was an extraordinary security measure, used only in situations demanding the highest level of protection and trust. Such precautions were necessary when safeguarding items of immense value or sensitivity, where access needed to be strictly controlled.

The use of two locks and keys ensured that no single individual could access the contents independently, requiring the cooperation of two trusted parties. This system guaranteed that even if one key holder was compromised, the contents remained secure unless the second key holder also colluded.

This setup foreshadows modern digital security systems, such as multi-factor authentication and public-private key cryptography, where multiple layers of verification are required to gain access. In both cases, the security mechanism is designed to prevent unauthorized access, ensuring that even if one layer is breached, the contents or data remain protected.

———————o———————

The year was 1650. Don Fernando stood on the ramparts of Portobelo, the white-topped waves crashing against the breakwater below. His eyes scanned the horizon, searching for the first glimpse of sails that would signal the safe arrival of the fleet. The wind was strong, pressing against his face as he walked. He knew that the wind, working with the ocean currents, should be guiding the galleons to a safe harbor.

The defenses of Portobelo, strong and unyielding, had kept the British pirates at bay, but he knew the battles at sea were different. They were unpredictable. His ships, heavy with goods and the burden of African slaves from Senegal, were more than just vessels of commerce. They represented the precarious balance of power and wealth he had carefully constructed in this remote, bustling colonial outpost. The wind and the sea had to work together, just as he and his allies did, to ensure success.

Portobelo, on the north coast of Panama, was a major center for the transatlantic slave trade. The demand for labor in the port and surrounding areas, combined with the influx of slaves brought to the Americas, led to a situation where the number of enslaved Africans in the town exceeded the number of white inhabitants by a factor of ten. The white population consisted mainly of Spanish officials, merchants, and military personnel. The enslaved Africans performed the bulk of the manual labor, including the handling and storage of goods, construction, and other physical tasks necessary for maintaining the port's operations.

Each day without the sight of sails deepened his anxiety. The seas between the Old World and the New were fraught with dangers: pirates, storms, and the ever-present threat of rival merchants. Yet, he held fast, knowing that this shipment could cement his standing as the most prosperous trader in Panama, a city quickly becoming the jewel of Spain's American empire.

Don Fernando's involvement in the slave trade troubled his friend Father Ignacio, but he found a way to settle his conscience. He had condoned the use of slaves to build his church, but eased his misgivings by commissioning a black Jesus statue. It provided the slaves with an idol to pray to after conversion. His church was, after all, in the business of saving souls. The condition of their bodies was out of his hands.

In the 17th century, while nations like the Dutch and British were building their empires through Protestant-led joint-stock companies like the Dutch East India Company (VOC) and the British East India Company, Spain's approach to its colonial empire was distinct and deeply rooted in its Catholic monarchy. Spain maintained tight control over its colonies through direct royal authority, and trade, including the slave trade, was centralized under the crown rather than delegated to private enterprises. This centralized approach was steeped in irony, as the Catholic Church, with its teachings on human dignity and the sanctity of life, coexisted alongside the brutal realities of the transatlantic slave trade. Don Fernando's rise within this system was aided by his noble connections in Seville, which secured him a lucrative position as an administrator within the Spanish slave trade. Yet, the irony lay in his ignorance of the dark legacy behind his appointment—likely secured through family ties complicit in the very trade he now oversaw. Despite his Catholic faith, Fernando remained unaware, or willfully ignorant, of the deep contradictions between his religious beliefs and the role his family and his position played in perpetuating the horrors of slavery. This paradox highlighted the complexities of a Catholic empire that justified its conquests and economic exploits under the guise of spreading the faith, while engaging in practices that starkly contradicted its moral teachings.

Spain's system, unlike the relatively more privatized Dutch and British models, was a stark reminder that the intertwining of faith, power, and economic gain often led to moral compromises. These compromises would shape the course of history, leaving individuals like Fernando both beneficiaries and victims of a system that was as hypocritical as it was powerful.

The only details Fernando knew of the trade were that slaves were captured in various parts of West Africa and transported across the Atlantic in horrendous conditions on slave ships. This journey, known as the Middle Passage, was infamous for its brutality and high mortality rates. The slaves destined for Panama were unloaded in ports like Portobelo and Nombre de Dios, key points in the Spanish Main, the network of Spanish colonial territories along the Caribbean coast. From these ports, they were distributed to various parts of the colony, including urban centers and plantations. Fernando's concern was for the movement of working bodies, not their welfare, but occasionally he found comfort in talking to Padre Ignacio, whose concern was spiritual. Each found it comforting to blot out the unsavory aspects of their roles.

Padre Ignacio, a devout Catholic deeply ingrained in the doctrines of his faith, easily reconciled the suffering inflicted by his church with his own spiritual peace. With the unwavering approval of the Spanish crown, Ignacio dismissed the brutal realities faced by the slaves who were forced to build and maintain the church while being compelled to convert to Christianity. His strict religious upbringing had trained him to overlook the harshness of colonial life, focusing instead on the loftier visions of heaven and hell. In his mind, the suffering of others, particularly those without the Church's protection, was merely a reflection of their sins—a divine justice meted out by God. With the Pope and the Catholic monarchy as his moral compass, Ignacio believed that his place was not to question the system, but to accept and enforce it, viewing the misfortunes of the enslaved as a necessary prelude to salvation in the afterlife.

Don Fernando summoned Padre Ignacio several days after the arrival of his latest fleet—a heavily armed convoy that sailed regularly between Spain and its colonies, bearing goods, silver, and other treasures. Though the convoy had miraculously navigated through the dangers of pirates, privateers, and hostile European fleets, he felt a sense of unease that even their successful arrival couldn't dispel.

"Padre Ignacio," Don Fernando began, his voice betraying the gravity of the situation as he welcomed the priest into his private chambers. "Please, take a seat. We have a matter of utmost importance to discuss."

"Thank you, Don Fernando," Padre Ignacio replied, his tone carefully measured. "I had been forewarned that such a meeting would be inevitable given the circumstances that have unfolded."

Don Fernando leaned forward, his gaze sharp and intense. "As you are well aware, the Archbishop of Panama shares responsibility with the Governor for the governance of this colony. Normally, I would have consulted with both of them regarding such a delicate matter. However, I have reason to believe that a higher authority in Spain has decreed that this issue is to be handled solely by you and me, and no one else. At least, for now."

Padre Ignacio nodded, a glimmer of apprehension in his eyes. "Indeed, I received a similar message. The special envoy from the captain of La Fortuna de Alba delivered a package to me yesterday with explicit instructions to bypass all customary procedures. It was to be handed directly to me and no one else."

"Interesting," Don Fernando mused, glancing at the ornate box placed prominently on the table beside them. A shaft of light from the setting sun fell on one of its cast iron handles. "Over there, you will see a finely crafted box, adorned with intricate inlay and secured by two locks. Such a strong box would normally bear the crest of the sender, but this one has no such signature. It arrived under similar instructions—bypassing customs and all formal channels. But there is more. I received a second, much smaller package aboard a different vessel. I have already opened it, and it contained a key that operates only one of the locks on this box. My understanding is that your package contains the second key."

Padre Ignacio hesitated, glancing at the package he had brought. "So it seems we are the only ones entrusted with the means to open this box. But why us? And what could be inside that requires such secrecy and dual authority?"

Don Fernando sighed; his expression unreadable. "That, my dear Padre, is what we must discover together. Whatever it is, it has been sanctioned from the highest levels. We must tread carefully, for even though we have been entrusted with this task, it is clear we are playing a dangerous game—one where the rules are known only to those far beyond our reach."

The two men exchanged a long, uncertain look, the weight of their shared responsibility settling heavily upon them. What lay inside the box remained a mystery, but both knew that its revelation could change everything.

They rose and stood before the box, their eyes enthralled by the intricate inlay work and the walnut veneer panels on top. It was not just a container; it was a statement, a piece of art designed to both impress and protect its mysterious contents. Slightly larger than a typical box but smaller than a chest, it exuded an aura of importance.

Don Fernando, holding the larger of the two keys, glanced at Padre Ignacio. "Shall we? No time like the present," he said, with the confidence of a man accustomed to practical solutions.

He inserted his key into the left-hand keyhole and turned it counterclockwise. A satisfying clunk echoed from within the mechanism. Fernando nodded to Ignacio. "Your turn."

Padre Ignacio, his face a mixture of reverence and caution, inserted his key into the right-hand keyhole and gently turned it counterclockwise. But instead of the anticipated sound, the key hit an obstruction halfway through. Frustration flickered across his face as he released the pressure and watched the key automatically return to its original position.

"It resists," Ignacio muttered, perplexed.

"Apply more force," Fernando suggested, taking the key from Ignacio and turning it counterclockwise. But the same resistance met his effort, the mechanism stubbornly refusing to yield and returning to its original position when the turning force was removed.

"It must have been damaged in transit," Ignacio said. "Perhaps we should summon a locksmith."

Fernando shook his head. "That would defeat the whole purpose of the plan. We're not fools. We can figure this out."

He fiddled with the lock, and after some effort, discovered that by holding the second key in the counterclockwise position, even without the reassuring clunk, the lid could be lifted. The second lock, it seemed, operated on a different principle from the first, yet the box was now open.

"How curious," Ignacio remarked, a hint of awe in his voice.

"Not curious," Fernando replied. "We simply didn't understand the maker's intent. There's logic behind every design, a reason for every mechanism."

"But we achieved our goal. The box is open. Why complicate it with unnecessary questions?"

Fernando sighed, shaking his head. "That's just like you, Padre. Always quick to see mysteries and miracles when most things have a rational explanation. If we understand how something works, we can better respond if things go wrong."

Ignacio responded, "But faith and acceptance are virtues too. Not everything can, or should, be explained."

"And yet," Fernando countered, "if there is a God, He gave us minds capable of questioning and understanding. If we didn't use those gifts, we'd still be in Spain, never having figured out how to build ships and navigate them across oceans. Progress comes from understanding, not just from faith."

The tension between them hung in the air, the box now open but the larger debate left unresolved—pragmatism versus faith, logic versus belief. Both men had their perspectives, but the contents of the box would decide which approach truly mattered.

As they peered inside the box, they were surprised to see very little. Their expectations had been to find a treasure of great value, perhaps gold, jewels, or a religious artifact aimed at feeding the faith and souls of the benighted. The sender, whose identity was still to be determined, had obviously gone to great effort to ensure that nobody had access to the contents and that only the key holders could view it. All they could see was a small wooden cross and a few letters and documents bound with a ribbon. It was immediately obvious that the importance of the 'treasure' lay in information.

Ines's letters, delicate and worn with time, revealed a love that had endured beyond the boundaries of life itself. In her cover note, she introduced herself as a young servant of a certain Duke, explaining that she had borne him a child—a son she could never keep. The Duke, bound by his position, could not acknowledge the boy as his own but arranged for the child's adoption and upbringing. Forbidden from returning to the Duke's household, Ines was left with nothing but the letters he sent her—a bittersweet connection to the life she had once known.

Two years passed, and the Duke visited her again. From this visit, another son was born, and like his brother, he too was adopted, but by a different family. Ines, though unable to ever see her sons, managed to keep track of their lives, her heart aching with the knowledge that she could never hold them, never whisper to them the truths of their origins. Yet, her love for them never waned, growing instead with each year that passed.

As she neared the end of her life, Ines's final wish was for her sons to know the truth—not only about their lineage but also about each other. She wrote not with bitterness, but with a deep, enduring love that had survived the years of separation. Her last letters, sent only when she knew she would no longer be alive to face the consequences, carried the weight of a mother's love—a love that could not be silenced, a love that would bridge the distance between her sons, uniting them as the only living remnants of her heart.

The two men stood in silence, absorbing the weight of the revelation. Their lives, once separated by an ocean and unknown to each other, were now intertwined by a truth that transcended mere coincidence. One was a dreamer, a philosopher whose soul sought meaning beyond the tangible world, while the other was a pragmatist, driven by the demands of reality and the pursuit of wealth. They were as different as night and day, yet the knowledge that they were brothers brought a new understanding.

The pragmatic brother, wealthy yet haunted by the fear of what lay beyond death, began to see in his brother's eyes a peace he had never known. The spiritual brother, though poor in material terms, carried a quiet contentment—a faith that death held no terror for him. He saw in his brother's hard-earned success a reflection of his own struggles, and for the first time, he questioned if he had been too quick to dismiss the value of the world he had shunned.

They realized that their lives, though divergent, were pieces of a larger whole. No one person could be complete on their own; it was through the balance of their contrasting natures that they found strength. The wealthy brother's cunning and ambition, paired with the spiritual brother's wisdom and compassion, formed a powerful bond that neither could have achieved alone.

What they shared went beyond mere respect—it was a bond forged by the understanding of their shared blood and the love of a mother who had sacrificed everything for them. They were not just two men coexisting in the same city; they were brothers, bound by fate and now by a love that transcended their differences. This realization didn't make them friends, but it created an unspoken connection—a brotherly love that, though unacknowledged, would guide them both in the years to come. When brothers don't exist, we need to invent them.

Glenn P. Wood,
York, PA
2 September, 2024

Post Script

The boxes described in these short stories are real antiques of historical interest selected from the author's collection of boxes, caskets and cases.

They are companions to the boxes whose stories are told in his preceding books:

'Messengers in Time' and 'Echoes from the Past'

Which are available through the usual retails outlets:

'The Art & History of Violin Cases'.

The Art & History of Violin Cases follows the development of violin cases from the 17th century through to the present and even includes examples made by the greatest of all violin makers, Antonio Stradivari.

For further details regarding these or other historical boxes, feel free to contact the author directly at: glennpwood@yahoo.com

Who is Glenn Wood?

Glenn grew up in Southport, England, and later studied Philosophy and Chemistry in the British universities of St Andrews and Oxford. His life shaping experiences include traveling extensively across Europe, engaging deeply with its cultural and historical treasures, and performing in Bolivia's National Symphony Orchestra.

He has explored ancient ruins in Latin America, Europe and Asia and accessed hidden collections of antiquities in China and Indonesia. Fluent in English and Spanish, he also speaks Several other languages to varying degrees and uses all them to communicate directly with the Antique heirlooms in his extensive collections.

Printed in the USA
CPSIA information can be obtained
at www.ICGtesting.com
CBRC090408041224
18174CB00098B/349